Writing

Short Scripts

Writing

Short Scripts

Second Edition

William H. Phillips

With a Foreword by Richard Walter

Syracuse University Press

The paper used in this publication meets the minimum
requirements of American Historical Standard for
Information Sciences—Permanence of Paper for Printed
Library Materials, ANSI Z39.48-1984. ∞

Phillips, William H., 1940–
    Writing short scripts / William H. Phillips ; with a foreword by
Richard Walter. — 2nd ed.
        p. cm.
    Includes bibliographical references and index.
    ISBN 0-8156-2802-1 (pbk. : alk. paper)
    1. Motion picture plays—Techniques. 2. Motion picture authorship.
    3. Short films. I. Title.
PN1996.P58 1999
808.2'3—dc21
                                                        98-53790

Manufactured in the United States of America

Still for Catherine Elizabeth Lostetter Phillips
(1899–1985)
who at age eighty-four last flew west
before the setting sun
bounded down steep airplane steps
and flashed fresh photos
of herself dancing at a wedding

WILLIAM H. PHILLIPS is a continuing visiting professor of English at the University of Wisconsin–Eau Claire. At the university level he has frequently taught short scriptwriting, introduction to film, and short fiction writing. He has also served as producer of readings of original short scripts for live performance then rebroadcast on cable TV. Phillips is the author of *St. John Hankin: Edwardian Mephistopheles* (1979), *Analyzing Films* (1985), and *Film: An Introduction* (1999).

Contents

Illustrations

Figures

Foreword

DOES THE WORLD NEED yet another book on writing film scripts?

As a screenwriting educator at a leading film school, I possess the authority to compel thousands of students to purchase such books. It should surprise no one, therefore, that publishers send me their latest titles at the rate of about two a week. Some stress creativity while others emphasize marketing. Some underscore visualization and others highlight plot structure. Some are lighthearted and breezy, others are ponderous, serious, and self-important.

But the one characteristic they all share—apparently without exception—is their focus upon the long form, the feature-length film that runs approximately one hundred minutes.

Virtually none treats the short film.

It is as if the short film represented merely a fringe within a far-wider universe belonging presumably to the feature. But this is, of course, a myth. In truth, the world of the short film—both creatively and commercially—holds far more possibilities for expression, to say nothing of production, than that of the feature.

For every feature-length film that is actually produced there are hundreds of short films. These include educational, instructional, and informational films; commercials and corporate image movies; travelogues; animated film; and short subjects covering a broad array of topics. And they include also the ever-burgeoning arena of student films.

So there is abundant reason to welcome the present volume.

First of all, it is certainly appropriate that a book about writing be well written. And William H. Phillips writes with clarity and insight, offering advice that is not only theoretical but also useful in a hands-on, shirtsleeves sense. This is uniquely affirmative in so practical an enterprise as film.

Moreover, the precepts and principles Phillips proposes are provocative and pertinent not exclusively for film writers specializing in the short form but also for filmmakers, the whole cast of artists and craftspeople who are the writer's collaborators.

And perhaps best of all, William H. Phillips recognizes that in all creative expressions, including film, what is significant is not the way things come apart but how they come together. Differences among various phenomena pale beside their vast, shared, common areas. To its author's credit, this book focuses not upon the differences but the similarities.

For, as is asserted implicitly throughout this book, there are two—and only two—types of films. And these are not short films and long films. Rather, they are good films and bad films. This book is for writers and film artists who are eager to produce films belonging in the former category.

RICHARD WALTER

Preface

THIS BOOK IS DESIGNED to help you write effective short scripts that have a good chance of being made into films or videos. Although many of the book's suggestions and guidelines apply to feature-length scripts, the book emphasizes writing scripts of fewer than thirty pages.

I have written this book for beginning scriptwriters, would-be filmmakers and videomakers, and students required to write short scripts or make short films or videos. Those planning to work for the professional short-film industry or to write feature-length scripts will find this book helpful in getting them under way. People planning to make their own short fictional films or videotapes will find the book will save them time and money and help them bring to life what they have to show.

The best short films and short scripts usually have one or two major, unchanging characters seen during a brief story time (usually a few days or less), who have one goal (usually unspoken) and who encounter several obstacles in trying to reach it. Although short films and feature films have much in common, they differ in several important respects. Most feature films contain one or more major, changing characters seen during a story time that may be weeks, months, or years, with two or more major goals and many obstacles to overcome, some of them involved and time-consuming.

Feature scripts are so complicated that most scriptwriters should model their first scripts on effective short scripts and short films. As it is better to write short stories before writing a novel, so it is better to write short scripts before tackling a feature-length script. The chances of finishing and finishing well are much increased if you complete short runs before attempting long ones.

Most effective short scripts are based not on television shows and movies but on events that writers know well and can re-create vividly: their own experiences or the experiences of someone they know well. To capture some of those experiences in writing, beginning scriptwriters will find it helpful to write journal entries and do writing exercises as they study short scripts and short films. Before they write scripts, they need to understand a writer's goals, the importance of visuals, the possible functions of dialogue, and the components of fictional stories. Next, they should plan, write, and rewrite their scripts, then seek readers and listeners, and eventually producers.

As I did research for this book, I used the following sources: McIntyre Library, University of Wisconsin–Eau Claire; Library, California State University, Stanislaus; Margaret Herrick Library, Academy of Motion Picture Arts and Sciences; Library, American Film Institute, Los Angeles; Library and Film Center, Museum of Modern Art; Billy Rose Theatre Collection in the Lincoln Center Branch and the Film Department in the Donnell Branch, New York Public Library; Audio-Visual Center of Indiana University, Bloomington; AV Department, South Bend, Indiana, Public Library; and the University of California Extension Media Center in Berkeley. Both the Sundance channel and Independent Film Channel have proven excellent sources to study recent short films.

Martin F. Norden of the University of Massachusetts, Amherst, shared his excellent home page with its many links to sources for screenwriters, which is cited in the bibliography.

Godfather to this book has been Richard Walter—Screenwriting Chairman, the Department of Film/Television at UCLA—who has been its enthusiastic and valued champion.

Writing
Short Scripts

Telling a story to convey feeling and experience is . . . as natural to man and as vital to man, and as intuitive and ageless . . . as to embrace when in love and to flee when in fear.

—ROBERT CRICHTON, in Olivia
Bertagnolli and Jeff Rackham, eds.,
Creativity and the Writing Process, 152

Part One

Getting Started

Relationships between girls and boys and men and women are used repeatedly in fiction, and there are hackneyed situations that you should avoid. But in most cases you can find a safe path by asking these two essential questions: What really happened? And what was there about the action, the thoughts, the outcome that was truly unique? Of course there are those situations which at first glance seem too close to clichés to be credible or interesting. Occasionally lovers really do patch up quarrels while standing on the shore of Lake Placid under a full moon in June. But not often. You may have to douse the moon, change the name of the lake, and give the characters some uneasiness about that reconciliation if the story is to take on a sense of authenticity.

—STEPHEN MINOT, *Three Genres*, 128

Finding Sources

Good story ideas can come from anywhere . . . but the best can be plucked from the family tree. More than fodder for amusement, these stories bring relatives and friends closer together and are a bridge between generations. "When an old person dies," Alex Haley once told the national storytelling league, "it's like a library has burned down."

—DIRK JOHNSON,
"A Storytelling Renaissance," 19

ALTHOUGH PROFESSIONAL SCRIPTWRITERS often write successful scripts based on extensive reading about a subject, you should base your first short scripts in part on your own experience or the experience of someone you know extremely well.

In teaching scriptwriting, I have seen many students write effective stories based on significant experiences they know well. One student story, for example, was based on the tensions between a lonely and protective mother, her daughter who lives at home yet goes to college and works part-time, and the daughter's boyfriend, who is eager for her to move in with him. The writer knew that material firsthand and presented it vividly and convincingly. Another story worked because its male author could give convincing details about the powerful, mostly sexual feelings a young man had for an attractive young woman and about his insecurity, awkwardness, and possessiveness that finally drove her from him.

Use experiences that show something interesting about life. Begin with character and story. Do not begin with an idea then look for characters and a story to illustrate it. Rarely does a writer begin with an idea—for example, a person can be both good and evil simultaneously—then write a vivid and convincing story. Beginning with an idea then writing the story usually results in an illustrated lecture, not the believable illusion of significant experiences from life. Most stories based on people and events that have not been part of the writer's life fail. Especially unlikely to have the right details are stories about characters older than the writer, of the opposite sex, or about characters in an occupation or lifestyle unfamiliar to the writer.

A student once showed me an outline for a story about a business executive, airplane pilot, and flight attendant who survive a plane crash. In conference, I asked him what experience as a business executive, pilot, or flight attendant he had and when he had survived a plane crash. When he replied he had no such experience, I asked where his words and images would come from.

Without thorough knowledge of your subject—gained either by experience or occasionally by thorough knowledge of someone else's experiences—your story will quickly reveal that you have only a passing acquaintance with its subject. You may not realize this until you've invested much time and effort—and become increasingly unwilling to abandon a story doomed at conception.

I told the student who was considering doing the story on the airplane crash and the survivors that I suspected his language and images would come from commercial television and films—perhaps vaguely remembered. What is wrong with those sources? The material you borrow from probably isn't true to life, and even if the material is effective, you will probably outfit it in the wrong clothing and spoil the effect. In an interview, Neil Simon said, "You see bad movies, bad television things, and you say, 'God, this is awful.' The reason it's awful is that it doesn't come out of any truth; it comes out of the imagination of some not-very-talented writer who is more likely imitating something he saw in the movies or on television rather than something he saw in life" (Brady 1982, 334). Your scripts should imitate life, not someone else's imitations of it.

Media stories are not a promising source for your first short scripts: they describe experiences that you do not know well and probably could not make your readers and viewers believe in. For example, I once read a newspaper account of a man who killed a young man and woman and was then caught and convicted. The fathers of the murdered man and woman were witnesses at the execution. At the last moment, the murderer asked for their forgiveness. One father nodded his head that he forgave. The other did not. This experience might be included in a larger, powerful story showing the results of both forgiveness and the inability to forgive. Few writers, however, even professional writers, could take this incident from the newspaper, write it into a script, and make us entirely believe in it. The script would lack the right details. Using media accounts as sources for your first scripts may not work because such accounts often deal with situations whose causes and consequences you may not understand. (You might collect fascinating media accounts and occasionally draw from this well for details in your scripts.)

In your scripts you should also avoid irrelevant violence or sex. One day I was walking in Central Park when I heard shouts and swearing, turned my head, and saw a heated argument. Even in New York, where loud confrontations are not unheard of, the argument stopped a few people and drew stares. Five minutes later into the park, I saw a couple lying on the grass embracing and kissing. That, too, is a common sight, but it attracted attention. Violence or the threat of violence and sex attract attention. You know that, and filmmakers have known it from the beginning of cinema. The trick is to use violence and sex only if their use is consistent with the characters in your script.

This caution also applies to profanity and obscenity. If they are appropriate to the characters and situation, then use them. But remember that profanity and obscenity are spoken violence. Stephen Minot compares sex and violence to electrical voltage. Too much in a frail wire and you burn it out. The shorter the story, the less tension it can carry without turning into melodrama, soap opera, or unintentional comedy. (A feature film is more like a cable and can carry much more sexual and violent voltage.)

A short film that attempts to carry too much voltage is *Strange Fruit* (briefly described in Films and Videos). During the film, the following actions take place in a small 1948 Georgia town:

1. A black minister who is encouraging blacks to register to vote confronts a white sheriff who doesn't want them to vote.
2. The main character, a young African-American man, finds the minister's body.
3. The main character nearly comes to blows with a friend who was taught by the minister so that he could pass the voter registration test.
4. After the main character attempts to register to vote, he is beaten up by several white men, put into handcuffs, and arrested for disturbing the peace.
5. After the main character is released, he is caught and beaten by a mob of white men.
6. His mother finds him hanged in a tree.
7. Two white men enter the back of a black church where the main character's funeral is in progress, but the black people show defiance and pride.

All this could have happened in 1948 life, but it's a bit much to accept in a thirty-two-minute film. *Strange Fruit* has as much violence and tension as some feature-length films. Although the film is well acted, filmed, and edited, and is sometimes moving, it lacks the force it might have had because of too much voltage in too frail a wire. By attempting to show too much too soon, the film seems calculated and a little desperate to make its points.

Avoid using experiences that are too recent or too painful because you may lack a clear understanding of them. Writer-director David Seltzer said, "I count on my memories. . . . But I want to get far enough away to experience them as a story instead of as real life. Then I can focus on the characters and what's happening to *them*" (Scheuer 1986, 27). The death of a loved one or divorce or separation, for example, can be excellent subjects if enough time has passed to allow you to see the experience with some objectivity.

If you write about a recent or painful experience, you may not select the most significant events and may not omit insignificant details. You may also take it personally when readers or viewers tell you their responses to the characters. As Marsha Norman advises, "Don't write about your present life. You don't have a clue what it's about yet. Write about your past. Write about something that terrified you, something you still think is unfair, something that you have not been able to forget in all the time that's passed since it happened" (1988, 407).

In your short scripts you should also avoid daring or dangerous experiences. Car chases, explosions, falls, pistol shots, acrobatics on moving trains, even fistfights are all dangerous to film or videotape. It's also difficult for nonprofessional filmmakers or videomakers to make such actions believable; in fact, the results are often laughable. Leave such actions to the professionals. Another reason to avoid these actions is that, although they are commonplace in action movies, they would be out of place in your first, more personal short scripts, which you should base on experience and life as it is lived outside movie theaters.

Yet another subject to be wary of is pets. Notice that I said above to choose an experience that shows something interesting or important about human behavior. Occasionally, beginners make a pet the central character in a script. These animals may be important in a person's life and a story drawn from it, but pets should not be the central characters in a script. Yours may be important to you emotionally, and some of that emotion may be important to a story, but the pet's noble qualities and sad death should not. No pet is nearly as fascinating as a person. (I know, I know, some pet owners will disagree.)

A final type of experience not suitable as a subject for your story is unbelievable happenings. What if a short film or video showed a woman being shot in a holdup. As the doctors prepare her for surgery, the bullet, which passed through a fur coat and three sweaters, falls out. Soon after, as the woman's mother rides a subway home, she overhears a fourteen-year-old boy boasting that he had recently shot a woman. The mother follows the youth from the train into a restaurant, where she calls the police. Although the boy disappears after the police arrive, the mother finds him while searching the streets, and the police arrest him. As it turns out, a police officer arresting the youth lives next door to the family whose daughter had been shot! Imagine you saw this as a short film or video. The audience would groan and boo, don't you imagine? Yet it's true ("Talk" 1985, 8).

Such events happen. We all had incredible experiences and

know of unbelievable ones. And it's tempting to use them in stories because they are fascinating. But if they are presented in a fictional story, they will be doubted. As the above newspaper account illustrates, truth is often stranger than fiction; truth is often harder to believe. You must tell a story that readers and viewers will believe, one that does not distract them with questions about its likelihood. It's futile to defend an improbable story by saying "but it really happened." That something happened doesn't matter. That it will be believed as a story does.

In summary, your short script should originate from one of your believable yet significant experiences that is not too recent, and it should avoid dangerous actions, unmotivated and irrelevant sexual or violent acts, and unnecessary profanity and obscenity.

Although your script should begin with an experience you know well, it should never end there. You must transform the experience into a fictional script.

Often in conferences students show me a few scenes based on an experience, but they don't know how to write a complete story. To take an example, a student once showed me an episode based on material she knew well. A man separated from his wife leaves her and their children after a visit. Soon after, one of the young daughters accidentally sets fire to a curtain then denies it. The mother questions each child separately. When the guilty girl's turn comes, she finally admits the deed. The student had presented the events vividly, but the story was only an anecdote, not effective fiction.

I suggested that the student change the names of the characters in the story to fictional ones and that she consider the following possibilities: What if the script shows that the girl started the fire because she was distracted by thoughts of her father? What if she started the fire because she was angry about and preoccupied with her parents' breakup, for which she feels partly to blame? What if the father returned after the girl's confession and treated the incident as unimportant because he believed it would ingratiate him with his daughter and annoy his wife? What if the daughter saw through the father's strategy and came to the defense of her mother? What if the other children were angry with the girl because her initial denial caused them to suffer a painful cross-examination by their mother and they wanted to get even with their sister, who started the fire? What if the mother overreacted to the burned curtain because she was upset (the father's presence upset her, maybe being a single parent was getting her down, perhaps she still loved the man and wanted him back)? What if the mother said she forgave the daughter, but by her actions showed that she was still angry—or preoccupied with the father?

I suggested that the student add some of these possible actions to the original anecdote and show the causes and consequences of the burning of the curtain. Additional significant actions and dialogue of this family will show more about them and let us discover some of their complexities. The writer has only to ask *what if* . . . then see what might be revealed about the characters.

To begin to get a perspective on an experience, it often helps to change the names of the people and to make other changes, such as omitting a person or adding an incident that didn't happen. The writer is then more likely to start creating fiction, not report life.

Fragments of autobiography rarely make satisfactory scripts. Life is too unfocused, its significance often unclear; its minute-to-minute experiences too humdrum to long keep audiences gazing at a motion picture or video screen. As Alfred Hitchcock supposedly said, drama is life with the dull parts left out. Successful writers know to cut, transform and rearrange events, and change and invent characters. No wonder films and videos can be so special. They can show us more, show it in sharper focus, and do so more quickly than can life itself. For a representation of how writers create fictional stories, see figure 1.

David Huddle writes, "When you sit down to write, you discover that *one thing leads to another,* and that in the act of writing, you can recover many fragments of your life that have been lost to you; you can begin to recover whole chunks of your history. 'It's all back there somewhere,' one of my informed friends told me, tapping the back of his head. If you think about that bedroom curtain, you remember, of course, that it was green, that it had a musty smell . . . that your mother made it, that she made matching bedspreads for you and your brother, and that you would stand beside the sewing machine and talk with her sometimes while she worked . . . and, and, and . . ." (quoted in Bertagnolli and Rackham 1982, 106–7; final ellipses Huddle's).

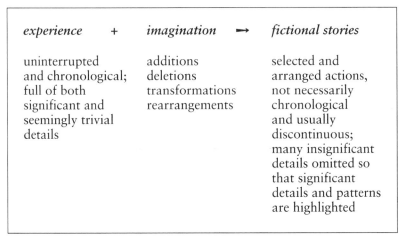

experience	+	imagination	→	fictional stories
uninterrupted and chronological; full of both significant and seemingly trivial details		additions deletions transformations rearrangements		selected and arranged actions, not necessarily chronological and usually discontinuous; many insignificant details omitted so that significant details and patterns are highlighted

Fig. 1. The making of fictional stories

Before you write, consider *when* you should write.

You should write when you are rested. "Giving up as little as one night's sleep seriously undermines the mental skills of spontaneity, flexibility and originality that enable people to change perspective and break out of established thought patterns" (Stevens 1989, B7). Write, then, when you are rested: good writing demands the best you have.

You should write during your productive time: in the morning (if you are a morning person) or in the evening (if you thrive at night). If you are a morning person, try getting up every morning at least thirty minutes early and write before you talk to anyone, read anything, listen to the radio, or watch television. If you are a night person, try to write for at least thirty minutes each night without interruption.

Writing after doing exercise can also be especially productive. Henry David Thoreau talks about that in his *Journal* of 19 August 1851: "How vain it is to sit down to write when you have not stood up to live! Methinks that the moment my legs begin to move, my thoughts begin to flow, as if I had given vent to the stream at the lower end and consequently new fountains flowed into it at the upper. . . . The writing which consists [exists] with habitual sitting is mechanical, wooden, dull to read" (1906, 8: 404–5). Because exercise can stimulate creativity, before your day exhausts you, jog, walk, run, swim, lift weights, or do an alternative exercise. Chuck Loch, a psychologist who has studied writers' creativity, says, "Anything physically repetitive, distracting or slightly boring will do" (1981, 21). While exercising, you may experience a surge of images, ideas, and energy; you may find memories and feelings you thought were lost. If ideas for writing come to you as you exercise, you can either try to remember what you want to write or carry along a tape recorder or stop exercising and write. It's a hard choice, but much better than lacking something to write.

One of the best ways to capture your experiences and imagination in words is to keep a journal or notebook and write in it nearly every day. If you use a loose-leaf binder, entries can easily be entered, taken out, rearranged. If you write with a computer, you can also store your printouts in a loose-leaf binder.

In both journal entries and writing exercises, described below, be sure to skip every other line, so you'll have room to rewrite. Some writers crowd what they have to say onto the pages, leave no room to rewrite, then *don't* rewrite. After all, there's no room! Don't allow yourself that excuse.

Below is a sample journal entry called "The Day Dad Moved Out," which was written by one of my former students, Melinda Cornwell:

> We shared a duplex—green faded paint with white trim—with foreign neighbors who brewed fish heads all day long. That's what Mama said anyway.
>
> "I've had it, Bill." I can still hear her. "I can't listen to promises anymore."
>
> He filled the dirty white sedan with his stuff. A torn plaid suitcase into which he threw all his man's things—razor, pocketknife, unfiltered Camels. Running a hand through his military haircut. Smelling of smoke, soap, and beer.
>
> "Kiss your old dad now," he said.
>
> Someone kissed him. It wasn't exactly me anymore. See, it had all been decided. Nothing I could say or do could keep him from leaving. He might even yell at me. So I just stood there an awful, awkward minute.
>
> "I'll send you a new coat when I get there."
>
> My eleven-year-old wrist bones poked out of the one I was wearing, a green corduroy whose sheen had rubbed off.

Of course, he never sent a coat. I didn't miss the fighting. But still. Some part of me went into that shabby plaid suitcase, drove off in that dirty white car.

In your journal entries, try to follow three guidelines.

First, show people talking and interacting. Re-create in words what people said and did. That's the stuff of life and the mother of stories. To keep your journal entries vivid, severely limit the time and place you re-create. Note in the above entry that except for the last paragraph, the entry portrays experiences that lasted only an hour or so and took place in or near a duplex.

Second, show, don't tell. Don't, for instance, explain that what you write is funny or sad; write in such a way that the entry *is* funny or sad. One student wrote a journal entry describing a cemetery where adults held each other in grief or stood alone, while children ran and plucked flowers from graves once surrounded by somber adults. Unfortunately, the writer went on to explain what the scene had already shown—that the children represented life. Such explanations can insult and alienate readers.

Finally, in your journal entries use concrete words instead of abstract or vague ones, such as *beautiful, nice, very,* and *brave.* For instance, through dialogue or descriptions, reveal that something or someone is *beautiful*—whatever that means; don't claim a person is and expect to impress your readers. Use specific words that show what experiences looked and sounded like. From your writing, readers should be able to see and hear what you had in mind.

Some other tips on journal entries:

1. As you write your journal entries, do not worry about spelling and punctuation. Do not worry about possible errors. Concentrate on getting into words what was said and done or what something looked like. If you eventually use the journal entry, you can correct it later. Besides, worrying about errors as you write is bound to stifle your creativity.
2. Use separate paragraphs for separate speakers.
3. Try to show what happened, not to impress your readers.
4. It's hard to be precise about the length of a journal entry, but one

to two single-spaced pages (typed) or two to four typed double-spaced pages seem the usual length.

Types of writing you might include in your journal:

1. events that stick powerfully in your memory, such as
   a. an argument that changed a relationship you had or have,
   b. a perplexing experience you suffered through,
   c. an experience that led to a surprising conclusion,
   d. an experience that showed you for the first time something about people (for example, that *your* best friend could betray you)
2. dialogues that reveal what people are like
3. outlines or summaries of stories that show how people behave

Do not include entries about what you did recently or what you are currently worried about or thinking over. For the reason explained above, do not describe *recent* happenings or your *recent* thoughts. For now, those will usually prove poor sources for stories.

Some writers believe that it's important to jot down what they have to say as soon as possible. Others, such as Woody Allen, say that you will remember the good stuff. Still others use a portable tape recorder for at least part of their journals, but with those machines you are selecting and recording, not writing.

Remember, if you like, this journal is for your eyes only, so be candid about what you write. You may eventually find parts of your journal useful in a script, or you may combine parts of the journal and discover a source for a scene or story. If not, you are at least looking and listening and writing. You are getting in shape.

Writing Exercises

Writing exercises, which are more structured than journal entries, sharpen your skills and help you find materials for scripts.

The nine writing exercises that follow should be kept in your journal or notebook and reread from time to time but not immediately after you write them.

1. Focused Freewriting. Write quickly and spontaneously about an experience you had or know well. As you write, record whatever comes to mind without worrying about sentence structure, grammar, spelling, capitalization. Don't worry about the possible usefulness of what you scribble. Above all, don't judge what you write or try to rewrite it as you write. Don't worry, just write. When your attention begins to lag, rest for a few moments; then write some more.

   If you freewrite on a computer, try turning off the monitor, or turning it down so far you cannot see what you write. That way, you are less likely to be distracted by your writing. You are less likely to be drawn to negative thoughts, less likely to want to redo at once what you write. Negative thoughts and rewriting while you write strangle creativity.

   When you finish, put this exercise in your journal but do not look at it for a few days. When you read it, you may find effective passages; you may not, or at least you don't think so now.

   This exercise may help you tap your unconscious, the well of most effective imaginary writing. You can never predict how productive focused freewriting will be. And you may do this exercise for a week or two and be convinced it is a waste of time. For most writers, though, the exercise eventually produces some effective writing. Some writers use it when they have trouble getting started writing or restarted.

2. Write everything you can remember about an experience that made you react emotionally: anger, jealousy, sadness, longing, pride, whatever. Describe the location, sounds, and events. What happened? Write the details without much planning or order. When you finish, put the passage aside for a day. The next day, reread it and add details that come to mind. Then rearrange the material into chronological order.

3. If you have a family photo album or set of slides, look at the album or slides. Choose photos that evoke strong feelings, and write about one of them. What was happening? What did it look like? What did it sound like?

   As you continue to look at a photograph and write, forgotten memories may flood your mind. Your past may live again. Write it all down without revising, and later see if any of it might be useful in a story. If it doesn't seem so for now, put this exercise into your journal and look at it again another day.

4. One day when I was about twelve, I was riding my bicycle near the former drawbridge entry into the port of Corpus Christi, Texas. On the shore, three feet below the bank, sat two of my friends. I pedaled down the bank at top speed, approached the edge above their heads, shouted to them, slammed on the bike brakes—and flew right over their heads into the shallow water. The bike frame was bent, a watch my father had given me was torn from my wrist and lost, and I was soaked, confused, and trembling. From that experience I gained a sudden and deep-felt realization: I was subject to the laws of nature, jarring surprises, indignity, injury, even death—especially if I acted recklessly. After that, my life did not seem so charmed.

Choose an experience that taught you something about yourself or about another person you know well. Or choose a series of closely related events that changed you. (Possible subjects: the time you learned you are more—or less—violent or impatient or poised or whatever than you had thought before. Or, a time you became disillusioned with someone.)

Do not describe and analyze the experience, as I did my experience above, but re-create it in words. Be sure to give specifics. Where did it happen? How? With what consequences? Show, don't tell.

After you have written a first draft, read it aloud at least twice and revise.

5. Choose an experience about which you have mixed feelings, such as love and hate (or love and indifference), joy and sadness, fear and excitement, desire and disgust, exhilaration and depression, or anger and forgiveness. Change the names of the people involved and re-create the experience in one or more scenes of action and dialogue.

As you later revise this exercise, remember that a scene is usually part of a larger action. For example, a scene showing a couple breaking up should not include all of their final conversation but just enough of it to indicate what is happening. After you have written the scene, you will probably discover that you need to prune the beginning or ending or both.

6. Imagine two characters having a dialogue, and they are both tense. Reveal that tension through dialogue and action, but don't have them push or punch each other.

   After the first draft, rewrite the dialogue: take out unnecessary words and sentences and reword phrases. At this point, add descriptions of gestures and indications of tone of voice where they are needed. Be sure that the indications of tone of voice are necessary: beginning writers often explain how performers should deliver their lines when the dialogue itself suggests how they should be said. Your dialogue should seem natural yet should be more compressed, interesting, and revealing than real conversation. Above all, it should reveal what the characters are like.

   After you have done two or more drafts of the dialogue, have someone read one part aloud and someone else read the other. As you listen, take notes; then revise.

7. Write a scene that presents three people you know well in conflict or under pressure. Be sure to indicate what they do and what they say, but do not reveal how you feel about them.

   Change names, possibly change the order of events, omit unnecessary details, add others. The result should be a scene with believable action and dialogue.

   Revise and file in your journal or notebook.

8. Secure permission from two or three people to tape-record their conversation for half an hour. Next, transcribe five to ten consecutive minutes of the most interesting part of the conversation. From the transcription choose a couple of pages that best convey their personalities. Last, rewrite, condense, and focus the conversation so that it conveys much in few words yet still seems natural.

   Some writers eavesdrop on people then re-create their dialogue. Others consider that practice an invasion of privacy. You decide that one.

9. Many scenes in films contain no dialogue. Actions and settings show us what characters and places are like.

Study the descriptions of *Avenue X* and *The Resurrection of Broncho Billy* in chapters 5 and 6; then write a scene of your own without dialogue that shows something about a character. Use the same format as the one used in the cutting continuity scripts for *Avenue X* and *Broncho Billy*. Be sure to include only *concise* descriptions of locations, times, and actions.

Part Two

Studying Scripts and Films

You can mess up a good script and make a bad film, but I don't think you can make a good film out of a bad script.

—DAVID LEAN, director, in videotape, "Hollywood Screenwriters and Their Craft"

I think short films are very necessary . . . to the cinema because it's [the] research department of the cinema, and without the shorts you can't learn, you can't try, you can't be innocent, and you can take risks in short films that are more difficult to take in [the] long feature.

—JACO VAN DORMAEL, director, National Public Radio, 19 March, 1992

Screenplays

STUDYING BOTH SCRIPTS and films is essential for the developing scriptwriter. Unfortunately, few film scripts are published in English, fewer still of short films, and when short scripts are published, they tend to be adaptations of famous short stories and stay in print for only a brief time. Thanks to two major film cable channels, with short films the situation is better though far from ideal.

In the following pages I include three original unproduced screenplays that are based on believable human experiences that the writers knew well. Films made from these scripts would require no locations difficult to reach or re-create, no unreasonable demands on the actors, and no special effects. Also included are two scripts that describe successful finished films. All five scripts are used as examples in chapter 7 of the scriptwriters' goals and means to attaining them.

As you read the screenplays (chapters 2–4) and study the two scripts that described finished films (chapters 5 and 6), remember the observations made in the introduction about the components of most effective short scripts: one or two major, usually unchanging characters seen during a brief story time (usually a few days or less); one (unspoken) goal; and several obstacles.

Each of these scripts is in the master-scene format: each numbered scene describes uninterrupted action in one location.

That's What I Love about You
Screenplay

MELINDA CORNWELL WAS born in Cortez, Colorado, in 1958. She "has two sons and has wrecked two cars." Her work has been published in *Apostrophe, Penumbra,* and *Writing Short Scripts* (first edition). It has been performed at California State University, Stanislaus, and at the Unity Church in Merced, California. She currently writes reviews of spiritual books and is active in several community organizations.

Before she wrote the screenplay reprinted below, she had written a journal entry about the main situation treated in the screenplay. You may find it useful to read it both before and after you read her screenplay, to understand some of her sources and what she made of them.

Journal Entry: "A Little Remorse"
Melinda Cornwell

Thinking of writing about Mama's operation and how it brought us closer. I was seventeen and Missy had just turned sixteen. The surgery was for thyroid, technically minor—but not in the minds of two young girls who had already lost their father through divorce.

She was already over fifty. The procedure was rough on her. I remember the lurid scar like embroidery floss across her pale, hanging neck. The clear tubes feeding into her nose, her hand. We went to see her as much as we could stand, then home to each other.

I washed a lot of dishes. Missy smoked a lot of cigarettes, openly, tossing the crumpled packs of Marlboro Lights one atop the other till the trash can teetered with them.

We'd get into the beat-up white Volkswagen and drive to the park minus the beer. I knew she drank with friends. We'd sit with the lights off and radio on, its glowing red strip the same color as her cigarette.

Or we talked, never about the really major things:

I'm afraid she's gonna die.

I'm sick of worrying about her since Daddy left.

What's gonna happen to us?

Instead we talked about guys, the ones I pined for, the ones she got arrested with. We talked about writers. For her report card, though dotted with Ds and Fs, never failed to contain the word "potential." "Melissa is brilliant but she seems a little remorse," one teacher wrote, oddly. Mama and I decided he meant "remote," but as the years go on, I'm now more convinced he had it right.

"Shit, you're so pompous," she said. "*Read* Hemingway before you decide he sucks."

It took me a decade to do that, and even longer to admit I *had* been pompous. About guys she was wrong and still is. But our adult love for each other took form on those parked, worried, cigarette nights.

THAT'S WHAT I LOVE ABOUT YOU
Melinda Cornwell
To Missy, with love

1. INT. HALLWAY OF THE GEORGE HOME—MORNING

It is a small, older house. Laundry spills from a hamper. Mrs. George stops her seventeen-year-old daughter, Sylvia, speaking as she puts on earrings, zips up dress. She is small, with protruding eyes.

MRS. GEORGE
I want you to wake your sister.

SYLVIA
Oh, God.

MRS. GEORGE
She's missed three days this week already. The school secretary called

MRS. GEORGE *(cont'd)*
again. And meat for dinner—put
something out now or you'll forget.

SYLVIA
What dinner? She won't be here to
eat it.

MRS. GEORGE
She'd better be. I have enough to
deal with. I shouldbe in the recovery
room late this afternoon but don't-
worry about me. Just make sure
your sister gets to school.

SYLVIA
Yeah, right.

Mrs. George steps into bathroom.

MRS. GEORGE (O.S.)
I'm not getting any sick days for
this. I'll be home the minute they
let me up. Carol says you can call
her if you need anything.

SYLVIA
I know.

Mrs. George steps out of bathroom, putting on shoes.

MRS. GEORGE
I've gotta go. Bye, honey.

She kisses her daughter perfunctorily. Sylvia hesitates,
then changes her mind.

Studying Scripts and Films

SYLVIA

Bye, Mom.

2. INT. GIRLS' ROOM—MORNING

Rock posters cover the walls. One side is neat; the
other features dirty clothes and used ashtrays. On the
messy side, Lisa lies face down in bed in her clothes, covers twisted around her, snoring. She bears some resem-
blance to Sylvia but has a muscular, heavier body and
much larger breasts. Sylvia shakes her.

SYLVIA

Wake up, Lisa. I don't care if you
do have a hang-over. You're going
to school.

LISA
(drowsily)

Shut the hell up.

SYLVIA

Get up. Mom has surgery today.

LISA

Fuck off.

She covers her head, turning away from Sylvia.

SYLVIA

Did you hear me? She's having her
thyroid operation.

LISA
(confused)
Yeah? She gone yet?

SYLVIA

She just left.

LISA

Goddamn it. Why didn't you wake
me?

Sylvia just looks at her. Lisa sits up, fumbles for a cigarette, smokes.

LISA
(continuing)
So . . . They're gonna cut on the
old bag's neck. Maybe they'll keep
going and take her head off.

SYLVIA

That's what I love about you.
Your compassion.

Sylvia turns to dresser, pulls out jeans and socks, and
gets dressed as they speak.

LISA

I wish they'd take mine off. Listen,
I'm droppin' by Randy's after
school.

SYLVIA

School! For God's sake, you don't
have to keep up the pretense.

LISA

Shut up. I feel like shit. She left,
huh?

                    SYLVIA
        Very good.

                    LISA
        Y'know, this'd be a great time to
        kick your ass. She wouldn't even
        know for two, three days.

                    SYLVIA
        I'm frightened.

Her eyes do reveal some fear.

                    LISA
        Damn right. So . . . Ya want a ride
        or what?

                    SYLVIA
        No thanks.

Lisa looks at the clock.

                    LISA
        You'll be late, Miss Priss.

                    SYLVIA
        At least I'll get there.

Sylvia collects books and purse, gives her hair a quick
last brushing, and leaves. Lisa flops back onto bed.

3. INT. HIGH SCHOOL LIBRARY—MORNING

Suzanne, Beth, and Sylvia sit at a table, books open, talking intently. Suzanne and Beth wear variations of
Sylvia's basic outfit, jeans and T-shirt.

> SUZANNE
> Did you guys see the dress Debbie
> Kistler has on?

> SYLVIA
> I guess that explains her, uh, bois-
> terous reception at the rally. I
> wasn't looking.

> BETH
> Must be nice to get such an eager
> welcome.

> SUZANNE
> Yeah, that's what half the foot-
> ball team said.

They all laugh maliciously.

> BETH
> You guys done on Taylor's thing?
> Pick a state capital? (They groan.)
> Might as well get it over with.

They reach for books and work a few seconds silently.

> BETH
> (continuing to Sylvia)
> What's goin' on with your mom?
> I mean, you could stay at my
> house . . .

> SYLVIA
> No, that's OK. Um, she'll be home
> in one or two days. It's—I'm fine.

                    BETH
                  (doubtful)
   OK.

                   SUZANNE
   I told her she could stay with us.

Suzanne and Beth exchange a look.

                    BETH
   Hoping Robby-poo will call?

                   SYLVIA
   I told you they're getting ready for
   his sister's graduation. They've
   got a lot of shopping to do and
   stuff.

                   SUZANNE
   I just—what if Lisa and Randy
   trash the house or start, uh, doing
   it in the living room or something?

                   SYLVIA
   I'll just tell her it's her funeral.
   But they have.

                    BETH
   They <u>have</u>? In the <u>living</u> room?

Librarian approaches their table.

                   LIBRARIAN
   Girls, keep your voices down or
   I'll have to ask you to go outside.

SYLVIA

Well, almost. Actually it was the laundry room.

SUZANNE

You're <u>kidding.</u>

SYLVIA

I wish. I'm going out to put my gym clothes in the dryer and there they are, for God's sake, on top of the washer with their pants down. And when I told my mom, Lisa said, "You know how bad his eyes are, Mama. He fell in the mud and I was putting his pants in the washer." <u>Right.</u>

All laugh. Sylvia's look turns to disgust.

SYLVIA
(continuing)
I just can't believe what my mom lets her get away with.

BETH

I can't believe anybody'd get that desperate, to do it on a washer. Not very comfortable!

SUZANNE

I dunno. Robby's sister says once you have it, you get addicted. Then you have to have it all the time.

Pause. Fear and delight cross their faces. They resume working.

BETH

If my mom had to have surgery,
at least I've got Dad. You sure you
don't wanna stay over? I've got
the new Joni Mitchell tape.

SYLVIA

Yeah? The 8-track?

BETH

Well, cassette. I'm getting the 8-
track for my report card.

SUZANNE

You wish. Personally, I'll take Joe
Namath.

All of them except Sylvia laugh suggestively.

SYLVIA
(to Beth)

I'll be fine.

4. INT. CITY LIBRARY—AFTERNOON

Sylvia is working, pushing a loaded book cart and fill-
ing the shelves. She slows down at one section, her eye
caught by something. She takes out the book and begins
reading furtively. Its title: If Your Parent Dies.

5. INT. HOSPITAL ROOM—AFTERNOON

Mrs. George, sleeping, lies in bed with clear tubes feeding into her nose and hand. Across her throat is a
wide, bloodied gauze dressing. Lisa sits in a chair at
her bedside, crying loudly. Finally she blows her nose.

The trash can at her side is heaped to overflowing with Kleenex. The nurse peeks in.

NURSE

Are you still here, honey? Why
don't you go home for a while? I'll
call you the second she wakes up.

LISA

I—no. I better stay here. I, um, I
do need a cigarette, though.

NURSE

Does your mother know you
smoke?

LISA
(dryly)
Oh, yeah, she knows.

6. INT. GEORGE KITCHEN—LATE AFTERNOON

The room is a mess. Sylvia enters, sighs, sets school-books down on table, and begins to pick things up. She works a few seconds, then the door bursts open and Lisa enters.

LISA

Where the fuck <u>were</u> you?

SYLVIA

What does that mean?

LISA

She said she'd be in recovery
around three or four.

SYLVIA

I have a job, something you wouldn't
know about.

LISA

Oh, bullshit. You just didn't wanta
deal with it.

She lights a cigarette angrily and smokes.

LISA
(continuing)
Either that or you were hangin'
around here waiting for that
sorry-ass boyfriend of yours to
call. Which he won't.

SYLVIA

Well, all the really quality guys
were taken. Like Randy.

LISA

Shut up, bitch. I should kick your
ass for not going to see your own
mother.

SYLVIA

I'll get there! Somebody has to
clean this pigsty!

Sylvia busies herself again. Phone rings. She races to get it.

SYLVIA
(continuing)
Hello? (Her face falls.) Yeah, she's
here.

Sylvia hands the phone to Lisa. During the following conversation, Sylvia angrily washes dishes.

> LISA
>
> Yeah? (intimate laugh) Hi, babe.
> Yeah. No—I told you. My mom had
> surgery. No, I can't. (same laugh)
> You. I can't. My mom. Don't
> worry—it'll still be there, babe.

Lisa hangs up. She stubs out cigarette, throws wadded pack toward the trash can. It misses. She ignores it.

> LISA
> (continuing)
> I'm takin' off, Miss Priss.

> SYLVIA
> Going out to the laundry room?

> LISA
> If I had time, I'd kick it. You're
> damn lucky. If, uh, anybody else
> calls, I'm at the hospital.

> SYLVIA
> Tell her I'll be over as soon as I
> pick up the house.

> LISA
> Shit.

Lisa leaves. Sylvia reaches down for the discarded cigarette pack and sighs heavily as she throws it away.

7. INT. HOSPITAL LOBBY—EVENING

Sylvia walks in, approaches reception desk.

> RECEPTIONIST
> May I help you?

> SYLVIA
> I'm here to see Linda George. I'm
> her daughter.

> RECEPTIONIST
> I'm sorry. Visiting hours ended at
> 6:30.

> SYLVIA
> But I'm her daughter. Can't I just
> go up for a few minutes?

> RECEPTIONIST
> It's hospital policy. The patients
> need their rest. You can see her
> tomorrow from ten to noon.

Sylvia looks relieved. She turns and walks away.

8. INT. HOSPITAL CHAPEL—NIGHT

Sylvia is alone in the chapel. She flips idly through the
Bible, then puts it down. She paces around the room,
touching the crucifix, the stained glass window, the shelf
of religious tracts. She stands undecided for a minute,
then steps out.

9. EXT. PAY TELEPHONE OUTSIDE HOSPITAL—NIGHT

Sylvia scrounges in her purse for change, peering at
coins in the dim light, then dials.

                    SYLVIA
        Hi. Uh, is Rob there? (pause) It's
        Sylvia. (pause) Sylvia George. He
        took me to the fall concert.
        (pause) Yes, I will. (pause) He's
        not? OK. No, no message. Just
        tell him I called.

Sylvia sighs and hangs up. She stands before the phone
a second, depressed.

10. INT. GEORGE KITCHEN—NIGHT

Sylvia has removed all the canned food from cupboards
and is painstakingly putting it back. A roll of cut paper
lies on the counter. She sings over a tape recording of
Jackson Browne's "Doctor My Eyes."

                    SYLVIA
        Doctor my eyes . . . I cannot see
        the sky . . . Is this the price . . . for
        having learned how not to cry . . .

Door bursts open. Lisa enters. Sylvia is startled.

                    SYLVIA
                 (continuing)
        You could knock. Oh, I forgot. You
        would have to have an opposable
        thumb to do that.

                    LISA
            (grabbing Sylvia's collar)
        That's it, bitch! I've had it! You
        keep pushin' me! You're goddamn
        askin' for it!

She draws back her fist as a man would.

SYLVIA
(listlessly)
Like I care at this point.

Lisa shakes Sylvia.

LISA
I don't fuckin' understand you!
What if something goes wrong?
You never even made it over
there, did you?

SYLVIA
I don't want to discuss it.

LISA
You goddamn well better "discuss"
it! Who the fuck else do you
have—your snobby-ass friends? I
don't see them over here holding
your hand. And I hope ya enjoyed
your date with Robby. I heard
from Shelly Fields it's all you're
gonna get.

SYLVIA
(pauses)
Anybody can be popular if they
spend enough time in the laundry
room.

LISA
Will you give it a rest for just one
second? Have you thought about

LISA *(cont'd)*

what's gonna happen to us if
something happens to her? We're
talkin' about foster homes. Lisa
Gonzales was molested by three
different foster fathers!

SYLVIA

My heart's breaking.

LISA

Shut up! Has it ever occurred to
you that I might be worried about
your sorry ass?

SYLVIA

Sure, just like you're worried
about <u>her.</u> Coming in drunk—if
you come in at all. Screwing 21-
year-old guys. I hope you get pregnant.

Lisa slaps her. Sylvia cries with difficulty, chokingly.
Lisa looks away, awkward, slapping her pockets.

LISA

Where's my goddamn cigarettes?

She finally finds one, lights it, smokes furiously. Her
hands are shaking.

LISA
(continuing)

This is my last pack. I'm gonna
have to go to Circle K.

Phone rings. Lisa gets it, talking angrily over her sister's sobs.

> LISA
> (continuing)
> Yeah? Yeah, it's me (pause) Not now, goddamn it! (pause) Yeah, I still love ya. I'll call ya. (pause) Yeah, yeah.

She hangs up and turns to Sylvia.

> LISA
> (continuing)
> So now what? You finished, or what?

> SYLVIA
> How dare you say I don't care about her?

> LISA
> I know, I know. You're sensitive as hell. That sorry-ass letter from Cornell's 'sposed to prove it, I guess. I thought about tearing it up, but shit. They'd just send ya another one. Mama's little trophy.

> SYLVIA
> You don't get it, do you? <u>You're</u> the one she loves.

> LISA
> Oh, right. Like the time she said to the police captain, "She can rot in there. I'm not bailing her out."

SYLVIA

That was one time! What about the
forty times before that she <u>did?</u>
You're not here to see her cry!
You're not here to listen to her go
on and on "Where have I failed with
your sister?" Christ! Now I know
why Daddy drank.

LISA
(dryly)
I'm shocked at you, Miss Priss.

SYLVIA

I, uh, I didn't mean that. It's been
a long day.

LISA

I'm glad you said it. I was begin-
nin' to think ya had ice up your—

SYLVIA

You didn't have to hit me.

LISA

Look, I'm sorry, but goddamn it,
you had it coming.

Lisa checks inside her purse.

LISA
(continuing)
Yeah, I knew it. My last pack.
(awkwardly) Ya want to go with
me or what?

Sylvia hesitates.

> LISA
> (continuing)
> Come on. I'm not buying beer or
> a joint or anything. Besides, he
> won't call.

> SYLVIA
> I don't know . . .

> LISA
> She has her sleeping medication at
> eight. The old bag's out cold till
> tomorrow.

Sylvia looks relieved.

> LISA
> (continuing)
> Now get in the car before I break
> your arm.

11. INT. VOLKSWAGEN—NIGHT

The girls are parked at a convenience store.

> SYLVIA
> How'd she look?

> LISA
> Like hell.

> SYLVIA
> That's what I love about you. Your
> tact.

                    LISA
You were smart, man. When I saw
that bloody Band-Aid, I thought I
was gonna puke right there.

                  SYLVIA
You? The one who bench presses
how much? 250 pounds?

                    LISA
I near fainted. The nurse said,
"You better sit down, honey."

                  SYLVIA
You? Remember when you pulled
that 4-inch nail out of your foot?

                    LISA
Yeah, I just went, "I think there's
something in my foot." Then I
looked down. (pause) You want
anything? A Playgirl magazine?
(pause) Just kidding. I'll be right
back. (leaves and returns quickly)
I know—a pack of Trojans? You
never know when Robby'll be in
the mood.

Sylvia looks hurt.

                    LISA
                (continuing)
      Sorry.

Lisa leaves again. Sylvia sits, thinking.

12. INT. GEORGE HOME—NIGHT

Girls are at kitchen table, unwrapping Hostess chocolate cupcakes and eating them with Pepsi. The table also holds a bag of Cheetos and a bowl of chips. Lisa throws a wrapper toward the still-overflowing trash can.

> LISA
> (chewing)
> Good dinner, huh? You sure you don't wanna smoke a J? It'd be great. You might relax for once in your life.

> SYLVIA
> That's all I need. I'm up to receive my scholarship, and you stand up in the audience with a megaphone: "Hey, Sylvia George of 348 West K Street! WANNA SMOKE A J LIKE WE DID LAST NIGHT?"

They laugh.

> SYLVIA
> (continuing)
> You'd do it, too.

More laughter. Lisa wipes a tear away. Pause.

> LISA
> So, ya think she's gonna die?

> SYLVIA
> (shrugging)
> Why not? At this point, nothing'd surprise me.

LISA

That's what I love about you. Your
cheerfulness.

SYLVIA

I guess we just wait.

LISA

Yeah. Wait. (chews) Well, I tell ya
what. They'll have to go through
me to put you in some goddamn foster home.

SYLVIA

Thanks.

LISA

Randy and me'll just get married a
little early and you can live with us.

SYLVIA

Right. And wake every night to
groaning bedsprings. No thanks.

LISA

Uh, wait. That won't work. I for-
got he's still on probation. (pause)
She cries, huh?

SYLVIA

Almost every night. I don't think I
can take it much longer.

Sylvia grabs a handful of snacks.

                    LISA
        Well, maybe I'll hit a couple AA
        meetings. Randy's been on my
        ass, too. Like he should talk.

Lisa yawns and scratches.

                    LISA
                (continuing)
        I'm tired. I'm hittin' the sack.

                    SYLVIA
        OK. Goodnight.

She turns to table, then sink, cleaning up. Lisa turns at
the doorway.

                    LISA
        Last chance to smoke one.

Sylvia rolls her eyes.

                    LISA
                (continuing)
        <u>Fuck</u> the dishes, man. Just go to
        bed.

Sylvia hesitates.

                    LISA
                (continuing)
        I'll do them in the morning.

                    SYLVIA
        This I've gotta see.

                    LISA
You know, I still have time to kick
your ass.

                   SYLVIA
That's what I love about you. That
vast vocabulary.

                    LISA
                (playfully)
Yeah? How about these? Shit!
Piss. Gonads!

Lisa goes into the bedroom and can be heard yelling.

                    LISA
               (continuing)
Y'know, balls. By God, I should
know about those.

Sylvia laughs, exasperated. Pauses.

                    LISA
               (continuing)
Hey, leave a little light on, OK? I
might have to get up and take a
leak.

                   SYLVIA
Right. (pause) I will.

Focus on overflowing trash can.

                  THE END

Rock of Hope

Screenplay

ROSA MARÍA DÍAZ wrote: "By age twelve writing had become a very personal way to communicate what I couldn't say verbally. I grew up in central California and attended California State University, Stanislaus, where I got my B.A. in Spanish with a minor in Chicano Studies and where I discovered my special interest and career as a writer. I wrote several short stories and some short film scripts. My treatment for *Rock of Hope* was published in the first edition of *Writing Short Scripts*. Some of my writings were published by school publications and several of my poems have been included in poetry books. I am in the process of publishing my book of poetry. A couple of my songs have been recorded in Spanish and English, and I intend to have more recorded by famous singers in both languages."

ROCK OF HOPE
Rosa María Díaz

1. INT. PEDRO'S HOUSE, KITCHEN—EARLY MORNING

In the kitchen halfway lighted Pedro prepares a cup of coffee. His heavy footsteps echo in the quiet and dark house. Esperanza, his pregnant wife, stops at the door frame, looks at her husband, and goes up to him.

ESPERANZA
(indifferently)
You want me to fix you some
lunch?

PEDRO

No, I will try to come back for
lunch. (pauses and sighs) But,
there's so much to do. Right now
I'm leaving and I cannot wait for
you. You should've gotten up earlier.

ESPERANZA

But it's barely three o'clock. Right
now the sun doesn't come out until
six thirty or seven. You don't even
sleep comfortably, and you want
to leave already.

PEDRO

Doesn't matter. It's better that I
take a nap there, if it's possible.
The noise of the machinery will
wake me up anyway.

2. INT. CHILDREN'S ROOM—MORNING

Esperanza opens the half-closed door and walks in the
bedroom.

ESPERANZA

Victoria, Sarah, Lupe, Martín! Kids
wake up! You're going to be late
for school!

Sarah is awake but still in bed. She tries to hold in her
moaning but cannot.

SARAH

Mommy, I feel sick. I have terrible
cramps in my stomach. Can you
make me some tea? Mother, I don't
want to go to school.

ESPERANZA

You're probably getting sick
because Martín wet the bed, and
this cold weather makes everything worse. If we had more
rooms and more money to buy
another bed, Martín could be free
to wet the bed as often as he
wanted to. (sighs) But we don't
have either one.

MARTÍN
(jumping from the bed)
No. No. I didn't wet the bed. I
stopped doing that a long time ago.
You lie Mommy!

VICTORIA AND LUPE
(at the same time)
Don't call our mother a liar! Dumb
brat!

Lupe and Victoria look at each other with surprise, cover
their mouths with their hand, and laugh. Esperanza
looks at her sick daughter and touches her forehead.

ESPERANZA
Mija, are you cold? Let me cover
you up some more.

SARAH
(with tears in her eyes)
No, Mamá, I just feel too much
pain in my stomach.

VICTORIA
I think she's already starting her

VICTORIA *(cont'd)*
first stages of womanhood. That's
why she's so pale, look!

Lupe uncovers Sarah and there's a large dark bloodstain
in the bed.

MARTÍN
Oh, how sick! And I was sleeping
close to her, yuck!

Martín disappears out of the room.

SARAH
Mommy, what's that?

ESPERANZA
That means you became a young
lady. You're a big girl now.

Sarah looks confused.

3. INT. KITCHEN—MORNING

Esperanza has a bunch of fresh-cut herbs in her hand
and closes the back patio door to the kitchen. She puts
the herbs to boil with water and sugar. She wets a
towel under the faucet. Victoria and Lupe come in.
Esperanza walks back and forth in the kitchen.

ESPERANZA
Girls, go ask Mr. and Mrs. Sanchez
if they can take us to the hospital.

LUPE
But Mother, we're going to be late
for school.

ESPERANZA

What's more important, school or
the health of your sister?

She doesn't wait for the answer. She takes the wet towel
and goes into the hall.

LUPE
(making a bad face)
OK!

4. INT. HOSPITAL WAITING ROOM—MORNING

Esperanza and her children walk back and forth. The doctor arrives with Sarah by his side and smiles at Esperanza.

DOCTOR
(eyeing Esperanza's rounded belly)
Mrs. Rodriguez, your daughter is
fine. We gave her an iron supple-
ment. She has to rest, but she will
be fine. You can take her home—
and don't you worry now. Sarah
is young, but she's strong and
healthy. Try to relax. Forget all
your troubles. Think of the baby
you're carrying.

Esperanza hugs Sarah and smiles gratefully to the doctor.

ESPERANZA
I try to relax but it seems I can
never get rid of my problems. My
daughters tell me I am like my
own mother.

5. EXT. BACKYARD PATIO—NOON

Martín runs out the house looking for his father and finds him in the backyard. Martín hides behind some trees and from far he sees his father. Pedro sits on an old chair. He drinks. He bends backwards, straightens his legs, puts the bottle on the ground then puts his hands in the coat pockets. He looks around. He turns to the cloudy sky, closes his eyes, and tears roll down his face. After a few minutes he returns to an upright position, covers his face with his hands, and quietly cries. Pedro takes several sips of tequila. Martín is astonished and slowly walks up to his father.

> MARTÍN
> Daddy, what's wrong? How come you're drinking again? You prom- ised that you wouldn't do it ever again! Why, Daddy, Why?!

> PEDRO
> (hugging Martín)
> My son, you wouldn't understand why I drink. You're too young to understand life. (clears his throat) Now, go on, tell your mother to pre- pare some lunch.

Martín hesitates then leaves.

6. INT. ROOM BEHIND THE KITCHEN AND OPEN TO IT—NOON

Lupe, Martín, and Sarah are watching TV.

> VICTORIA
> Lupe, help me clean up this mess so I can vacuum.

LUPE

Move out of the way. I cannot see
the TV. Martín you should clean
up. It's your mess.

MARTÍN

Yeah, but Victoria told you. You
never do anything to help.

Martín stares at the TV. Victoria turns it off, and
Victoria, Lupe, and Martín all speak simultaneously as
Sarah looks on.

VICTORIA

Lupe, get up and clean your mess.
Martín, pick up your toys.

LUPE

Martín, pick up your toys. These
are my things that you got. Get
them in my room.

MARTÍN

You're not my mother to tell me
what to do. These are mine, but
you play with them, too.

7. INT. KITCHEN—SHORTLY AFTER NOON

SARAH

Daddy, I became a young lady. I'm
a big girl now!

PEDRO

And what does that mean?

                    SARAH
          That I can give orders, too!

8. INT. KITCHEN—DAY

    Pedro sits at the table. Esperanza cleans up the dishes.

                    PEDRO
          This morning when I got up, I
          heard one of the girls moaning. It
          sounded like she was sick.

                  ESPERANZA
          It was Sarah. My poor baby. She
          had her first period, and she was
          bleeding so much that she got the
          bed very dirty. I thought that she
          could bleed to death, so I took her
          to the hospital.

                    PEDRO
          Mm. Now I understand.

                  ESPERANZA
          The doctor gave her some medica-
          tion and some vitamins, but she
          will be all right.

                    PEDRO
          I wonder how can we pay the bills.
          I don't get paid enough for unnec-
          essary hospital bills. It seems that
          all my check goes to pay stupid
          medical bills, and they're not even
          mine.

    Esperanza turns to face Pedro.

ESPERANZA

I'm sorry I'm making you spend your money on us, but Sarah's condition needed medical attention. Our health is more important than the money or bills.

PEDRO

Of course, since you don't know what it is like to work, you don't worry how you spend the money.

ESPERANZA

And you think that the housework is a game? It's a job like yours, but I don't have breaks and don't get paid either.

PEDRO

That's why I have told you to go back to Mexico. Looks like you want to take revenge on me. Look, we can have this house rented, and with that money you buy another one over there, and I know you'll live more in peace.

ESPERANZA

You think everything is that easy. And where do you think we would stay while all that is being arranged? And where would you stay?

PEDRO

I can stay under any tree.

ESPERANZA

But certainly! What you don't want is to have obligations. But I am happy we are here with you so you can see it's not easy being a parent of four kids. And just think, we're going with the fifth child.

PEDRO

Look! I'm tired of listening to the same comments every day! If you had stayed in Mexico a while longer, we probably had a nice house by now, and maybe even a small family business. That's all I ever wanted!

ESPERANZA

Yes, you only talk about what you want. What about what the kids want? If I had listened to you, the children couldn't be in school. Instead they would be working from sunrise to sunset.

Pedro stands up and walks to lean on the counter, lowers his head, and shakes it saying no.

PEDRO

Why do you think I work so much? It certainly is not for pleasure but to support you guys.

Esperanza walks around the kitchen cleaning various things.

ESPERANZA

For years I suffered alone caring
for the children. I got tired of
being a mother and father while
you were here so carefree just
sending money. Then you decide
to send for us so we all can have
a better life, and now that we're
here, you want us to stop spend-
ing money in medical checkups.

PEDRO

If you guys go back to Mexico, you
can have a good life and soon I can
join you. A dollar over there goes
a long way. Here it's only a dollar.

Esperanza stops before him and places a hand on her waist.

ESPERANZA

Everything has the same value
here or there. And I won't move
from here. Like it or not, we're
here, and you have obligations
towards the kids and I, too.
(raises her tone of voice) We both
had the kids and that's why I
came here so we can both care for
them!

Pedro slaps Esperanza twice.

PEDRO

I am tired to hear you're a mar-
tyr. I am tired that you only count
your suffering. I am tired of your
solemn attitude.

Esperanza falls to the floor fainted. Pedro gets on his knees and places her head on his legs.

> PEDRO
> (continuing)
> Esperanza! I'm sorry. Oh, God,
> what have I done? Esperanza,
> Esperanza!

Victoria comes and finds her mother unconscious on the floor and her father trying to revive her. Victoria goes to her mother. She sits on the floor and cares for Esperanza but speaks to Pedro.

> VICTORIA
> You don't deserve to be called "a
> man." You're nothing but a cow-
> ard. Oh, yes, you can beat up my
> mother because she cannot defend
> herself, but you don't fight off
> the men in the streets that are
> looking for trouble! You're cynical,
> selfish! Beat me up too, I don't
> care. I hate you for this and many
> other things.

Pedro is ready to slap Victoria, but when his hand is about to reach her face, he slowly closes his hand into a fist and lowers it. A tear rolls down his face. He stands up and goes to the counter shelf, takes out the bottle of tequila, and pours a drink.

FADE-OUT

9. INT. HOSPITAL EMERGENCY ROOM—AFTERNOON

Esperanza has labor pains. A nurse comes to Esperanza's

Studying Scripts and Films

side and takes her temperature. Esperanza turns towards
the nurse and shows some bruises.

ESPERANZA
Nurse, where is my husband? I
have to see him. Please, call him
inside.

Esperanza lets out her screams of pain.

NURSE
Sorry Mrs. Rodriguez, your husband
doesn't want to come in. He says
that this is no place for him. He
will be waiting outside, in the hall.

Between screams of pain that go through the walls into
the hall, Esperanza shouts in her loudest voice.

ESPERANZA
Pedro, son of a bitch! You should
be here so you can see what I'm
going through! You're such a cow-
ard, stupid bastard!

10. INT. HOSPITAL HALL—AFTERNOON

The clock shows it's 5:00. Pedro sits on a bench, alone.
He closes his eyes and a tear rolls down his face. He
sighs and waits. The hour hand runs rapidly in the wall
clock and stops when it's 4:35.

11. INT. HOSPITAL PATIENT'S ROOM—EARLY MORNING

Pedro has a cup of coffee in his hand. He comes to sit on
the bench and drinks from the cup. He yawns and drinks
some more.

NURSE
Mr. Rodriguez, you can come and
see your wife now.

Pedro stands up, puts the cup in the garbage can, and
fixes his shirt and hair.

12. INT. PATIENT'S ROOM—EARLY MORNING

Pedro enters the room and sees his wife, who smiles
happily, holding their new baby. He walks in slowly.

ESPERANZA
Pedro, come closer. Meet your new
son. In spite of everything, he is a
healthy baby.

Pedro notices the bruises on Esperanza's face.

PEDRO
Esperanza, I am so very sorry for
what happened. I never meant of hit-
ting you. Everything happened so
fast. I . . .

Esperanza smiles at her baby with pride.

ESPERANZA
Hold the baby. He's so beautiful!

PEDRO
But he's so fragile. I'm afraid. I've
never held a baby.

ESPERANZA
Well, it's time. Children also need
of the love of their father. Here.

Studying Scripts and Films

ESPERANZA *(cont'd)*
The times we're living, this new
country, this new baby demand
that we change.

Pedro holds the baby. He smiles at the baby then at
Esperanza.

PEDRO
It's a miracle! Thank you for all
the children you have given me.

ESPERANZA
His name will be Roberto, like my
father.

PEDRO
No, his name will be Pedro, like
me, and José like my father.

ESPERANZA
I have followed every order and
accepted all the decisions you
make but not this time.

13. INT. HOUSE KITCHEN—AFTERNOON

Martín and Esperanza are at the table eating.

MARTÍN
Mamá, remember the day Sarah
got sick?

ESPERANZA
Yes.

MARTÍN
When I went outside looking for
Daddy, I saw him crying. He

MARTÍN *(cont'd)*
always says that boys don't cry.
Why did he cry that day, Mommy?

ESPERANZA
I don't know <u>mi hijo.</u> But I can find
out.

MARTÍN
OK, Mommy, but don't say I told
you, please.

Martín leaves through the door, and Pedro comes in from
the back door. He sits at the table across from Esperanza.

ESPERANZA
Why haven't you been to work in
the past few days?

Esperanza stares at Pedro.

ESPERANZA
(continuing)
The weather is getting warmer,
and there should be more work.
But you look so carefree.

PEDRO
I haven't been to work because they
laid me off. But I think they won't
call me back because I've heard
rumors that the rancher is going
bankrupt.

ESPERANZA
Is it that, or the fact that they
found you drinking on the job, or

ESPERANZA *(cont'd)*
could it be that <u>you</u> want to change
jobs again?

PEDRO
I am telling you the truth, <u>Señora.</u>
If you believe me or not, that is
your decision!

ESPERANZA
All your life you've changed jobs like
you change socks. And the kids are
the ones that suffer most. That's
why I have my doubts this time.
Anyway, what do you plan to do?

PEDRO
I guess I plan to be a migrant
worker like I've always done. But
before you object, let me tell you
what I mean.

Pedro stands up and walks around the kitchen.

PEDRO
(continuing)
I want to go to the nearby ranch-
ers and ask for jobs as fruit picker.
Like today I can pick oranges, next
time are walnuts, then tomatoes.
Whatever is available. But everything has to be in this area. And
most important of all, I want to
make a garden out of the backyard. Whatever I plant, we can sell
it later. How's that sound to you?

Esperanza shakes her head in disagreement.

14. INT. KITCHEN—AFTERNOON

Pedro comes into the kitchen where Esperanza is. He calls the children to come into the kitchen.

> PEDRO
> Sit down, we're going to have a lit-tle discussion!

The children roll their eyes and contort their mouths knowingly. They take their time to sit down. They don't want to stay, but Esperanza, who is a step behind Pedro, winks at them in sign that they should.

> PEDRO
> (continuing)
> From now on, I am working every-where, doing anything and work-ing from sunrise to sunset if possible. But I want you children to help me out. On the weekends, holidays, and whenever you can come and work with me, picking fruit or vegetables. Working together we can save money and get out of this misery.

Pedro pauses waiting for a response. They all talk at the same time.

> VICTORIA
> We're going to get behind in school, and I am about to graduate.

LUPE
What will the neighbors say when
they see us all working?

SARAH
We won't have time or the energy
to do our homework.

MARTÍN
We are all too young to work. I
won't be able to play with my
friends anymore.

PEDRO
Look, people always criticize and
gossip because they are jealous. I
want to send you kids to school, to
college. I know Victoria wants to
become a doctor. Lupe wants to be
a teacher. Sarah wants to be lawyer.

Pedro turns to see Martín, kneels before him, and holds
him by the shoulders.

PEDRO
(continuing)
And you Martín, you haven't told
me what you want to be when you
grow up.

MARTÍN
I want to be a famous gambler in
Atlantic City!

Pedro puts his hand on Martín's head and messes up his
hair affectionately. They all laugh.

PEDRO

And how do you know of Atlantic
City?

MARTÍN

From the movies!

Pedro stands up.

PEDRO

Yes my son, you can be anything
you wish, but first of all, we have
to get out of this damn hole. I
never had the chance to study and
look at me. The only thing I know
how to do is pick fruit. All of you
have to study so you won't be
ignorant and useless like me. And
besides, you have to support us
in our old age.

Pedro turns to see Esperanza. She sighs and lowers her
head.

15. INT. LIVING ROOM—DAY

Lupe and Sarah finish decorating a Christmas tree with
a few ornaments. They search in boxes, but they're all
empty. They sit on the floor a bit disappointed. Martín
watches cartoons on TV. Esperanza and Victoria are in the
kitchen preparing dinner. Pedro arrives home a bit drunk.
He comes with a lot of gifts for the family. Smiling he
comes into the living room, puts all the presents on the
floor, stands up, tries to balance himself, then faces everyone, pointing. Victoria comes into the living room.

PEDRO

I am very happy. That's why I
went out to celebrate. Yes, we
have saved enough to do more
things which before we only
dreamt about. I have put all the
money in the bank, and today I
went to check how much we had.
You know how much we have?

Pedro is tumbling, so he stops talking to balance himself.

PEDRO
(continuing)
Ten thousand dollars! With all the
interest it has added to ten thousand dollars.

The children jump for joy. Victoria gets closer to Pedro.

VICTORIA

Father, I am sorry for being so
rude to you. We see you so strong
and proud that we think you can
take anything.

Esperanza comes into the living room holding the baby.
She puts him down on the floor and whispers to him.

ESPERANZA
Roberto, go, give a kiss to your
father.

The baby walks towards Pedro, but then he wanders to
the presents.

Rock of Hope

PEDRO
(sighs)
I know none of my children are bad.

Pedro and Victoria embrace.

PEDRO
(continuing)
Victoria will be attending college in
the spring. She sacrificed a lot by
helping me work and because
she's the oldest of my children,
she deserves the first chance.

The children don't wait any longer. They jump into the
presents.

FADE-OUT

16. INT. A CITY BAR—NIGHT

Pedro and three men are sitting at a table.

MAN # 1
Hey Pedro, what's up? We hardly
see you around here now.

Pedro pulls a chair to join them at the table

PEDRO
I've been very busy.

MAN # 2
Doing what? Watching TV?

Lets out a sarcastic laugh.

PEDRO

No! Me and my family are working together for one paycheck. And you know guys, it has worked.

MAN # 1

Really! Tell me then, why your family looks poorer than ever.

PEDRO

Because we're saving up to the last penny. And it has worked because we have several thousands of dollars in the bank.

MAN # 3

You hear guys, he's rich.

PEDRO

Seriously, we have saved around nine or ten thousand dollars in the past year. And with all this money Victoria will be attending college in the spring.

MAN # 2

Why do you want to send your kids to college? Especially the girls. They get married and then stay home.

PEDRO

But!

MAN # 3

Hey, you should buy yourself a

MAN # 3 *(cont'd)*
new truck instead. The one you
have now won't last too long.

MAN # 2
And if you get the new truck, you
won't have to worry if it will start
in the mornings to go to work. You
won't bother me again with the
jumping cables or other stuff.

MAN # 1
College can wait a while, but if you
don't have a car for work, you
don't have a paycheck either.

17. INT. KITCHEN—DAY

Through the kitchen window Esperanza sees Pedro
arrive. He gets out of a new truck. Esperanza is startled.
Pedro comes in happy calling everyone. The children
come in a group and right away they notice the different attitudes of Pedro and Esperanza. They crowd quietly in a corner and only their eyes move.

ESPERANZA
How come you went and got a car
if you deny us the right to buy
anything? You told Victoria she
could go to college and now you
spend the money on "unnecessary" things.

Pedro lowers his head angrily and sucks on his teeth.

PEDRO
No, no that's not it! The money is

PEDRO *(cont'd)*
still in the bank. I got this truck on
credit. I am tired of your constant
criticism. You people can keep
your money. I don't need it.

Pedro leaves the house slamming the door, gets in the
truck, and squealing the tires, leaves for the road.

18. INT. KITCHEN—NIGHT

Esperanza hangs up the phone shocked. Victoria comes
into the kitchen followed by Lupe and Sarah.

VICTORIA
What's wrong, Mother?

ESPERANZA
Your father is in the hospital. He
had an accident.

LUPE
Oh my God!

SARAH
We should go look for a ride.
Martín! Come on, let's go ask the
neighbors.

ESPERANZA
No, I'm calling for a taxi. We cannot be bothering people every time.

19. INT. HOSPITAL WAITING ROOM—NIGHT

Esperanza rubs her hands nervously.

ESPERANZA
Doctor, what happened? How is he?

DOCTOR
<u>Señora</u> Rodriguez, your husband
was driving drunk, hit another
car, and then crashed into an elec-
tricity pole. He suffered some
injuries, but fortunately, it's nothing very serious.

Doctor pauses; he hands a handkerchief to Esperanza.
She dries her tears. Victoria, behind her, holds her by
the shoulders. Esperanza cannot stop crying. She leans
forward and dabs at her eyes and sobs. The doctor
directs himself to Victoria.

DOCTOR
(continuing)
He was so drunk he didn't realize
what happened. You can see him,
but don't tire him out.

20. INT. HOSPITAL PATIENT'S ROOM—NIGHT

The entire family goes into Pedro's room. He's awake but
unable to move. He has scratches and bruises on his
face. They are all quiet and stare at Pedro.

VICTORIA
So, are you happy now? You are
destroying our lives! Because of
your drinking and your selfish-
ness, you have turned our lives
upside down. And you still expect
our respect for you?!

Pedro sighs and turns the other way. Esperanza pokes Victoria's arm to make her be quiet. Victoria pulls her arm away and raises her voice.

> VICTORIA
> (continuing)
> Don't you see that you two are the ones that keep this family together? And if you keep fighting any longer, this family will be shattered forever. You have to go to the Alcoholics Anonymous and also to a psychologist. In fact, we all have to go because we all are affected by your decisions.

Victoria starts crying. She moves back a few steps, and Esperanza moves closer to Pedro.

> ESPERANZA
> The cop said that the passengers in the other car came out well. But you will have to pay for all the damages because you have no insurance and it was your fault for driving drunk!

There is sadness in the silence.

> VICTORIA
> Father, you have the choice. You're still in time to change so we can become a real family. Because if you don't go to counseling, we will leave you forever!

Pedro sees a deep anguish in Esperanza, and although he can hardly move his lips, he says the following in a repentant tone.

                    PEDRO
          OK, I will go! I am also tired of
          this life. For the sake of this fam-
          ily, I will go and we all have to
          change.

Everyone gets around his bed. Esperanza takes the baby from Sarah, and he is happy and smiles at Pedro. Lupe, Sarah, and Martín sigh and smile. Victoria and Esperanza give a smile that hardly shows.

                                        FADE-OUT

                    THE END

The Road
Screenplay

ROBERT ORLANDO GRADUATED from the School of Visual Arts, completing his first short film, *See Her Run,* with a grant from the New York Council on the Arts. The film represented the school in the Tel Aviv Film Festival. After working as a freelance cinematographer and editor, he formed a production company and produced commercials, industrials, and documentaries, most notably the award-winning *La Famiglia,* the story of an Italian-American family. Orlando pursued a graduate degree in philosophy while writing short and feature-length scripts. In 1996, he was offered a contract for his film noir thriller *Madam Death,* which he hopes to direct as an independent film. He lives in New York as a writer and director and has completed three scripts, including a science fiction epic entitled *Emanon.*

THE ROAD
Robert Orlando

FADE-IN: Titles over the following montage.

1. EXT. CHURCH FAIR—NIGHT (MONTAGE)

A woman strolls through the festive surroundings of a church fair. Though her natural beauty is beginning to fade, her youthful eyes reflect the array of twinkling lights. She is holding the hand of the tall man beside her. They buy cotton candy, throw balls at milk bottles for prizes, and embrace in front of the carousel. Cecilia looks deep into his eyes. In the background plays "Are You Lonesome Tonight."

FADE TO BLACK

FADE-IN:

2. EXT. OPEN ROAD—DUSK

Stopped in traffic by severe flooding, beneath a thunderstorm is a huge flatbed truck carrying the parts for a carousel. The polished frames and painted faces of the mechanical horses are soaked with rain. From inside the truck, a radio reports a thunder and lightning watch. The road leads to a small town filled with bait and tackle shops, passing a sign that reads: The Only Road Through Meta Creek.

3. EXT. TOWN—SUNSET

Far removed from the ominous gray skies are the postcard images of a small town: brightly painted boats, wooden mailboxes, and vintage storefronts.

4. EXT. CHURCH—SUNSET

On the side of the road, a simple, whitewashed church sits alone in a tree-covered field. In the parking lot, men construct carnival booths and hang banners. There is a wooden sign on the grass with the painted announcement for the upcoming "Church Fair."

5. INT. DINER—SUNSET

From across the street, the woman seen during opening credits watches a boy through a camera lens, before

Studying Scripts and Films

snapping a picture. Stuffed in her apron pocket is a pad and pen, the uniform of a waitress.

The diner has an old country-style decor with a narrow aisle separating the tables from the counter. The calendar reads: June 6th, Meta Creek's Church Fair. The jukebox plays "Are You Lonesome Tonight."

> SANDY/FARLEY (O.S.)
> Cecilia! Cecilia!

She is called by the short and plump manager, Mr. Farley, and another waitress, Sandy. Formerly the town beauty, she now compensates with makeup and hairstyles.

> SANDY
> Cecilia! Cecilia!

> CECILIA
> What? (She turns her head and notices Sandy pointing at the customers with a telling facial expression) I know, I know.

> SANDY
> Can you stop lookin' out the window and help out and please stop playin' that song. It's givin' me a headache.

> CECILIA
> (Cecilia drops another quarter in the jukebox) Not tonight.

Sandy slides into one of the booths, holding a cold dishrag against her head. Looking through her lens,

Cecilia speaks.

>   CECILIA
>   (continuing)
>   You feel that way because you go
>   out with what's-his-name?

>   SANDY
>   (From under the rag)
>   Billy.

>   CECILIA
>   Billy. You get drunk, mess around
>   until mornin' then ya come into
>   work holdin' your head and yellin'
>   at me.

>   SANDY
>   Like you got somethin' better.

>   CECILIA
>   You should try stayin' home!

>   SANDY
>   By myself?! Are you crazy? This
>   girl is gettin' too old too fast.

Sandy recognizes Cecilia's gaze.

>   SANDY
>   (continuing)
>   Maybe for you stayin' alone is all
>   right, but I'm not sittin' around
>   waitin' for no prince charming.

>   CECILIA
>   It ain't a sin to be alone ya know.

Studying Scripts and Films

                    SANDY
You gotta get out a little more.

                    CECILIA
I know. I'm just waitin' for the
right guy.

                    SANDY
You mean the perfect guy.

                    CECILIA
Maybe.

                    SANDY
(Turns toward Cecilia) You say
that like some tall, dark, and
handsome man is gonna get off his
white horse and stroll into your
miserable life.

                    CECILIA
He already did.

                    SANDY
Would you forget about him
already. He ain't coming back, and
you'd better get used to it.

Cecilia grins as if hiding a secret.

                    SANDY
                 (continuing)
What happened to your big plans
to sell those pictures?

                    CECILIA
I will.

                    SANDY
        I don't see you goin' anywhere.

                    CECILIA
        I'm just waitin'.

                    SANDY
        You really think he's comin' back,
        don't you?

Cecilia lifts her camera to take another shot. Sandy
gazes at the boy.

                    SANDY
                  (continuing)
        Little Charlie out there again?

                    CECILIA
        Yeah. He's been sitting there for
        days.

Farley notices the customers craning their necks for ser-
vice. A pot burns on the stove.

                    FARLEY
        Ladies this ain't no social club!
        People come in here to eat, not to
        hear about your dirty laundry.

Sandy mimics Farley and walks off. Cecilia focuses
another shot of the boy. When the shutter snaps, the
stove bursts into a grease fire. Cecilia rushes to help.

                    FARLEY
                  (continuing)
        I can't have this in here! Every
        day it's somethin' else with you!

Studying Scripts and Films

Sandy puts out the fire.

> CECILIA
> I-I'm really sorry. I'm sorry.

Farley holds Cecilia's shoulders and speaks with a firm, quiet voice.

> FARLEY
> Cecilia, just go home.

6. EXT. PARKING LOT—TWILIGHT

Twilight has fallen over Meta Creek as Cecilia exits the diner. She is startled by the horn of a passing tractor trailer. Moments later, a pickup truck races into the parking lot, crosses her path, and comes to an abrupt stop. A chiseled man in his late thirties rolls down the window.

> JOSHUA
> Hey Cecilia, where've you been?

> CECILIA
> Nowhere. Around. I just ain't been
> much for drinkin' these days.

> JOSHUA
> You know, we could just go for a
> ride or somethin'. Maybe down to
> the creek. I got my boat all fixed up.

Cecilia approaches the car.

> CECILIA
> Josh, the truth is I just don't think
> we have that much goin' on
> between us.

> JOSHUA

Whadya mean?

> CECILIA

I just don't see us goin' anywhere.

> JOSHUA

I'm not talking about goin' anywhere. I'm talking about just bein'
together.

> CECILIA

That's just it. I don't want to . . .
"<u>just be together.</u>" Listen, just forget it.

Cecilia walks away.

> JOSHUA

Cecilia!

Joshua screeches out of the parking lot. Cecilia walks
across the road to little Charlie, seated beneath the lamppost. She stands beside him, sharing his gaze.

> CECILIA

Whatcha waitin' for?

> CHARLIE

My dad.

A car races past.

> CECILIA

Did he go away?

                    CHARLIE
          Hadda do business. Ya know . . .
          real important stuff!

                    CECILIA
          What does he do?

                    CHARLIE
          Drives a truck.

Charlie takes a swig of his soda.

                    CECILIA
          Can I have a taste of that?

Without removing his eyes from the road, Charlie hands
her the soda. Cecilia takes a sip.

                    CECILIA
                  (continuing)
          That hits the spot.

Cecilia searches his face.

                    CECILIA
                  (continuing)
          Where's your mamma?

                    CHARLIE
          Home.

                    CECILIA
          Does she know you're here?

Another truck passes, drowning out her words.

CECILIA
(continuing)
She know you're here?

Charlie shrugs his shoulders.

CECILIA
(continuing)
Where d'ya live?

CHARLIE
23 Whitewater Road.

Cecilia repeats the address under her breath, thinking.

CHARLIE
(continuing)
Dad can't cross the bridge, so I
wait for him here.

CECILIA
That must be a big truck!

CHARLIE
18 wheeler, Peterbuilt tractor, 15
speed. "Pull a pack of circus ele-
phants up the side of a mountain."

Cecilia smiles.

CHARLIE
(continuing)
That's what Dad always says.

CECILIA
And I bet you want to drive a
truck just like'm.

> CHARLIE
>> I drove it once, in Mr. Richards'
>> parking lot.

A tractor trailer approaches. The boy stands, makes eye contact with the driver, then pulls on an imaginary horn. The driver smiles and responds. After the honking fades, Charlie sits. Cecilia hands him the soda.

> CECILIA
>> Thanks for the drink. I'll see ya
>> later maybe, huh?

7. EXT. WHITEWATER ROAD—NIGHT

Later that night, Cecilia stops in front of a house with a decrepit porch. There is a small boy and girl sitting in miniature chairs. Cecilia cautiously approaches the front door, pausing to pat the small boy on the head.

> CECILIA
>> Is your mamma home?

The children avoid eye contact with Cecilia. She knocks on the door and waits. Country music emanates from a backroom, mixed with outbursts of laughter. Drawn by the sounds, she steps down from the front porch and walks around to the rear of the house.

Through an old screened window, Cecilia views a man and woman wrestling playfully on a bed. The woman's arms and legs are wrapped around the man, who is busily kissing her neck. When she notices Cecilia at the window, she pulls the sheets over her scantily clad body, then brushes the hair from her pretty face. The man is Joshua.

GENNA
Can I help you?

CECILIA
(Embarrassed)
I'm sorry; I didn't mean to—

GENNA
(Overlaps) What do you want?
(sarcastically) You can see I'm
busy!

After a moment of eye contact, Genna and Joshua burst
into more drunken laughter, falling back on the bed.

CECILIA
I came to tell you that your son
has been sittin' down at the gas
station all day.

Genna abruptly raises her head.

GENNA
I know where my boy is! How's
that your business anyhow?

CECILIA
Just thought you should know.

GENNA
Is that it?

Cecilia turns and walks away.

GENNA
(continuing)
Hey Miss!

Cecilia stops in her tracks.

> GENNA
> (continuing)
> Ya know, you shouldn't be pokin'
> your head into other people's win-
> dows (sarcastically) especially
> their bedrooms 'less you like that
> kind of thing.

There is one final burst of drunken laughter from Genna
and Joshua.

8. INT. CECILIA'S HOME—NIGHT

Cecilia is in her small home overlooking a nearby lake.
The living room is decorated with old furniture that sur-
rounds a fireplace. There are many homemade items
scattered about, including quilts, baskets, and fishing
memorabilia. Over a mantle is a wall covered with photographs. One picture is of a smiling man standing beside
an older man on a fishing trip.

The old man seen in the photo on the wall enters, holding his tackle box and fishing pole. He slams the door,
grumbling under his breath. Cecilia speaks from her
room.

> CECILIA (O.S.)
> Is that you Grandpa?

> GRANDPA
> Well, who else would it be? Why's
> everyone always screamin' around
> here?

Cecilia appears changed into a pair of denim jeans and

flannel shirt. While brushing her long hair, she stops to kiss him, then steps into the kitchen.

                    CECILIA
          Did ya catch anythin'?

                    GRANDPA
          Can't catch anythin' if ya don't
          do any fishin'.

                    CECILIA
          You didn't fish again? That's not
          like you.

                    GRANDPA
          Don't feel much like fishin' any-
          more. It was a lot more fun when
          your daddy was around (he stands
          beside the picture with his son).

                    CECILIA
          I'm makin' your favorite pota-
          toes—the way you like'm. Hope
          you at least worked up an
          appetite.

As Cecilia prepares dinner, the old man sets his fishing gear by the front door, then settles into an armchair by the fireplace. He gazes into the dwindling fire, listening to the rumblings of distant thunder.

                    GRANDPA
          Looks like we're gonna get a
          storm tonight.

9. INT. CECILIA'S HOME—NIGHT

Cecilia washes the dishes. Grandpa lifts the final log, placing it on the fire, then puts on his jacket and opens the door.

> CECILIA
> Where do you think you're goin'?

> GRANDPA
> Were gonna need more firewood
> with this storm comin'.

He grabs an ax.

> CECILIA
> Grandpa you're not gonna swing
> that ol' ax with your back. Doctor
> Reed said one more accident like
> last time and you're finished.

> GRANDPA
> Gus Reed? He should live as long
> as I have.

Cecilia throws the dishrag in the sink and rushes to her grandfather. She takes the ax from his hand, removes his jacket, then guides him to the armchair.

> CECILIA
> Sit yourself down. I'll just run
> down to the market and get us
> some firewood.

> GRANDPA
> You're not paying for firewood.

He tries to stand, but Cecilia holds him down.

                    CECILIA
            I told you not to worry about that.
            I have the money. What I don't
            have is another grandpa.

Cecilia kisses him on the top of the head, then puts on
his jacket.

                    CECILIA
                   (continuing)
            I'll be back in a bit.

                    GRANDPA
            Don't you go liftin' no wood.

                    CECILIA
            I'm takin' the wagon.

10. EXT. GAS STATION—NIGHT

Beneath a canopy of shifting clouds, Cecilia pulls her small
wagon into town. In the distance are flashing lights from
the closing fair, being shut down a section at a time. She
is shocked to find Charlie still sitting at the intersection,
his tired eyes fixed on the road. Cecilia approaches him.

                    CECILIA
            It's late. Maybe you should go
            home.

Cecilia stretches out her hand to check for rain.

                    CHARLIE
            My dad told me to wait for him
            here.

Cecilia scans the darkened storefront windows. The only light is the glowing neon from the diner.

> CECILIA
> (Cautiously) Does your dad live here with your mamma?

> CHARLIE
> No.

Cecilia sits in her wagon beside him. Occasionally, the hum of a car engine whirrs by.

> CECILIA
> What's your name?

> CHARLIE
> Charles Henry. My dad calls me "Snapper."

> CECILIA
> Why's that?

> CHARLIE
> He took me on a boat once, and I caught thirty-two snappers. You know snappers?

> CECILIA
> Baby blues. My dad was a fisher-man.

> CHARLIE
> We're gonna go fishin' when he gets back.

CECILIA
Your dad like to fish?

CHARLIE
Yeah. He always catches the biggest
ones! This is his hat.

CECILIA
That's nice. Sounds like you guys
do a lot together.

CHARLIE
Yep. When we go out in the deep
waters, he lets me stand on his
shoulders.

CECILIA
I know what you mean. I remember playing with my dad. He was
a strong man too.

CHARLIE
Strong?! (pulls his shirt over his
arm) My dad's arms are out to
here.

As Charlie gazes down the barren highway, Cecilia
breathes in the misty air.

CECILIA
Sounds like my dad.

CHARLIE
Where's your dad?

CECILIA
He's not around anymore.

CHARLIE
Where'd he go?

CECILIA
Heaven.

CHARLIE
Heaven? Is that in Meta Creek?

CECILIA
No. Well. Maybe. (hesitates) It's a
place where people go when they
die.

CHARLIE
How do you know he's there?

CECILIA
He told me he was goin' there. He
said we'd go fishin' someday. Go
out on the biggest boats and swim
as far as the eye can see . . . whatever we could dream of . . . that's
what we'd do.

Charlie notices tears in Cecilia's eyes.

CHARLIE
Why ya cryin'?

CECILIA
I don't know. I guess I miss him.

Cecilia forces a smile for Charlie while wiping her eyes.

                    CECILIA
                  (continuing)
        Charlie, there's a storm comin'.
        Would you let me walk you home?

                    CHARLIE
        I told you. I gotta wait for my dad.

                    CECILIA
        Did your dad leave today?

                    CHARLIE
No.

                    CECILIA
        When did he leave?

                    CHARLIE
I forget.

                    CECILIA
        Was it a long time ago?

                    CHARLIE
        He comes back every year.

After a silent moment, Charlie sips his soda.

                    CECILIA
        When was the last time you went
        home?

Charlie rests his head on his knees. Cecilia peers into the
lighted diner across the street. There is a woman using
the public phone.

CECILIA
(continuing)
I'm goin' inside to get somethin'
warm to drink. You want somethin'?

Charlie keeps his head down.

CECILIA
(continuing)
I'll be back in a bit.

11. INT. DINER—NIGHT

Cecilia flips through the phone book. Charlie is in view
across the street. After being hung up on, she slides into
a booth, overlooking the gas station. Mr. Farley
approaches her with a steaming mug.

FARLEY
You know you can't solve the
world's problems (grins).

She smiles warmly.

CECILIA
Don't want to. Just one little boy.

Joshua's pickup truck screeches into the gas station. It
abruptly stops in front of Charlie. Farley holds back
Cecilia.

12. EXT. GAS STATION—NIGHT

Charlie jumps up, wrapping his arms and legs around the
lamppost. Genna steps out of the truck, slams the door,
then marches toward him. Joshua looks the other way.

                    GENNA
          Now you get your ass in that truck
          right now!

                    CHARLIE
          No!

                    GENNA
          I said get in that truck!

                    CHARLIE
          He's comin'!

                    GENNA
          No one's comin'. Get in the god-
          damn truck!

When Genna tries to tear his hands away, Charlie hugs
the pole tighter. She slaps him across the face, drawing
Cecilia from the diner.

                    FARLEY
          Cecilia, he's not your child!

Genna's jaw stiffens.

                    GENNA
          Don't make me hit you!

Before Genna can grab Charlie, Cecilia steps in front.
Genna brushes the hair from her face.

                    GENNA
                 (continuing)
          What do you think you're doin?

                    CECILIA
          Just calm down. You're gonna
          hurt him.

                    GENNA
          What's it your business? Don't
          you got betta things to do than go
          around interfering with other peo-
          ple?

Genna drags Charlie by the arm back to the truck. His
fishing hat falls to the ground. With tears in his eyes,
the boy rolls down the window.

                    CHARLIE
          He's gonna come back! He won't
          know where to find me. Please!!
          Wait for him!

                    GENNA
          Close that window!

The truck screeches away, leaving Cecilia standing
beneath the lamppost in silence.

13. EXT. FAIR—NIGHT

Cecilia passes slowly through a turnstile, greeting a
wrinkled man holding an umbrella. Most of the booths
are closed, and the greater part of the fair sits in darkness. Only the pitter-patter of rain is heard as she wanders past the cotton candy stand and the familiar milk
bottle toss. Timidly, she passes small groups of men and
women standing in the shadows. They are counting
change and sipping from Styrofoam cups.

She approaches an empty lot with a sign that reads Carousel. The rain mixes with Cecilia's tears. In the background, there is muffled conversation that goes unnoticed by Cecilia. A tender hand reaches for her shoulder. She quickly spins around. It is her grandfather, who greets her with an embrace. She rests her head on his shoulder.

                    CECILIA
          Why'd you come?

                    GRANDPA
          I was worried about my little girl.
          I thought somethin' mighta hap-
          pened.

                    CECILIA
          (Wiping tears from her eyes) It's
          a long story.

                    GRANDPA
          C'mon. You can tell me on the way
          home.

14. EXT. GAS STATION—NIGHT

Soaked with rain, Charlie's fishing hat lies on the pavement. Cecilia steals a final glance down the highway as a huge truck approaches from a distance. After a brief hesitation, Cecilia and Grandpa cross the road, disappearing into the shadowy streets. The intersection is left in silence.

Moments later, the truck carrying the carousel pulls into the gas station. A tall man steps out of the truck near the lamppost and picks up Charlie's fishing cap. After squeezing out the water, he climbs back inside then drives away. From across the highway, Cecilia rushes toward the vehicle. She screams, but the sound of the accelerating engine drowns out her cries.

>   CECILIA
>   Wait! Wait!

15. EXT. ROAD—NIGHT

Cecilia chases the truck down the two-lane highway. A railroad crossing gate is lowered onto the road, forcing the driver to stop. Lights are flashing, bells ringing, and a long freight train is rumbling past. Cecilia leaps up to the driver's side, pounding the window.

>   CECILIA
>   Wait! Wait!

The man rolls down the window.

>   DRIVER
>   What's the matta lady? Lady?

>   CECILIA
>   Nothing.

>   DRIVER
>   You gone crazy or somethin'?

>   CECILIA
>   The hat . . . I thought . . .

As Cecilia steps off the truck, the driver tosses the hat onto the road. She crumbles to the ground as the red tail-lights vanish in the distance. The diner light goes out, leaving Meta Creek in darkness.

16. INT. DINER—SUNSET

The calendar reads: June 7th the Day After. The glowing sunset illuminates the evening crowd. Cecilia frames a shot of Charlie sitting in the gas station. After snapping a picture, Sandy appears.

                    SANDY
          Ya got any plans for tonight?

                    CECILIA
     Not again.

                    SANDY
          Just asking that's all.

                    CECILIA
     I have a <u>date,</u> all right?

                    SANDY
          (Surprised) Really? I know you're
          not going to tell me with who.

                    CECILIA
     No, I'm not.

Sandy recognizes a bag of peanuts and an orange soda on the table beside Cecilia.

                    SANDY
          Let me take a guess. It's with a
          younger man (smiles).

Cecilia gazes at Sandy, returning the smile. Preparing to leave, she notices her grandfather's pickup truck pulling into the gas station. It is loaded with fishing poles, tackle boxes, and bait.

17. EXT. GAS STATION—SUNSET

When Grandpa walks around the truck to fill it with gas, Charlie takes notice.

                    CHARLIE
          Hey mista, where ya goin'!?

Grandpa stands up straight, holding one hand on his aching back.

                    GRANDPA
          (Startled) Whad'ya say son?

                    CHARLIE
          Where ya goin'?!

                    GRANDPA
          (Under his breath) You don't have
          to shout. (louder) Gonna do a little
          fishin'.

                    CHARLIE
          Now?

                    GRANDPA
          (Looking at the sky) After that
          storm, they'll be mighty hungry
          tonight. Lucky if they don't eat
          the boat.

                    CHARLIE
          Ya gotta boat?

                    GRANDPA
          Sure do though it ain't much fun
          fishin' alone.

Grandpa fills the tank. After a short pause, Charlie approaches the truck.

> CHARLIE
> I'll go with ya mister, if ya want me to.

> GRANDPA
> You, son? It's gonna be pretty dark out there.

> CHARLIE
> I ain't scared.

> GRANDPA
> It gets kinda rough bringin' in those fish when ya can't even see 'em.

Grandpa gets into the truck.

> CHARLIE
> C'mon mister. You'll see what a help I could be. I always went out with <u>my</u> dad. You'll see.

Grandpa surveys the boy. Charlie runs around to the passenger side of the truck.

18. EXT. DINER—SUNSET

From the diner parking lot, Cecilia watches her grandfather and Charlie drive off. She looks at the hat, peanuts, and orange soda in her hands, then back at Sandy, now pressed against the window.

19. EXT. GAS STATION—SUNSET

Cecilia crosses the street and sits beneath the lamp-post. After opening the peanuts and orange soda, she frames a picture of the empty road with her camera.

Beams of light approach from a distance then pull in front of Cecilia. The driver rolls down the window.

                    SANDY
          You look pathetic.

                    CECILIA
          Thanks.

Sandy steps out of the car to sit beside her.

                    CECILIA
                  (continuing)
          What happened to your big night
          with . . .

                    SANDY
          Billy. Now how'd you expect me to
          have a good time with you sittin'
          out here?

                    CECILIA
          Now, don't go and ruin your night
          on account of me.

                    SANDY
          It's not just you. I've been doing
          some thinkin' myself—believe it or
          not.

                    CECILIA
          You?

                    SANDY
        (Jokingly) One thing's for sure.
        You're <u>not</u> a happy person.

                    CECILIA
        I suppose you are?

                    SANDY
        At least I got Billy.

                    CECILIA
        I meant <u>really</u> happy.

                    SANDY
        Things aren't perfect.

                    CECILIA
        C'mon Sandy. For once in your life
        be honest with yourself.

                    SANDY
                 (Overlaps)
        No one is <u>really</u> happy.

        They gaze down the quiet road.

                    CECILIA
        Look: you have what you want,
        and you're not happy. I <u>don't have</u>
        what I want, and I'm not happy
        either. Seems like we're both in
        the same boat.

                    SANDY
        Least I don't spend my time starin'
        down this empty road.

CECILIA

Who said it's empty?

SANDY

Ain't nobody showed up.

CECILIA

Yeah, you're right but sometimes
it feels good just hopin' someone
does.

As Sandy continues speaking, she reaches into the bag
for a peanut. Cecilia hands her the soda. The heavens
watch over the women's small frames, seated side by
side beneath the lamppost. The road is silent.

20. EXT. RIVER—NIGHT

Grandpa and Charlie float on Meta Creek watching the
still waters. Their reflection is a slow dreamlike shimmer.

21. EXT. ROAD—NIGHT

The carousel truck leaves the town, taking the polished
frames and painted faces of the mechanical horses. It
passes the sign that reads: The Only Road Through Meta
Creek, then speeds toward that place where the highway
meets the horizon.

FADE TO BLACK

FADE-IN: End titles over Cecilia's photographs.

Finished Films: Cutting Continuity Scripts

A CUTTING CONTINUITY SCRIPT describes a finished film; it may include shot and scene divisions, descriptions of settings and actions, dialogue, camera angles and distances, and sometimes even the duration of shots or scenes and the type of transitions between them. In the following two chapters we examine two such scripts, both in the master-scene format that you are urged to use in writing your scripts. If it is impossible to see the two films being described, don't worry. Close study of the following descriptions should prove useful in helping you understand the possible content and duration of scenes and what is left out of scripts. The different subjects, meanings, and styles of these quite different short films also illustrate some of the many options available to scriptwriters and filmmakers.

Avenue X
A Cutting Continuity Script
by Leslie McCleave

LESLIE MCCLEAVE GRADUATED from New York University's
Graduate School of Film and Television. *Avenue X*—which she wrote,
produced, and directed—was her thesis film. The film is set in the bleak
winter landscape of Coney Island, her favorite New York locale, and the
cast includes both professional and nonprofessional actors. *Avenue X*
won many awards including the first Excellence in Short Filmmaking
Award at the 1994 Sundance Film Festival, Prix Aaton at the Locarno
International Film Festival, and the Golden Gate Award for best short
narrative at the San Francisco Film Festival. The film also was screened
widely at festivals including the Berlin International Film Festival
(Panorama) and the Museum of Modern Art New Directors/New Films.
She wrote and directed a second short film, *Blixa Bargeld Stole My
Cowboy Boots,* which premiered at the 1996 Sundance Film Festival.
She's also directed several commercials and music videos and produced
a documentary for public television. Currently, she is New York–based
and developing two feature films, *The Shamrocks* and *ROAD.*

Avenue X, which runs 15 1/2 minutes, was made in 1993.

AVENUE X
A cutting continuity script by Leslie McCleave.

No reproduction or use of the following script and photographs is allowed without the permission of Leslie
McCleave.

Avenue X takes place in and around a fictitious seaside

neighborhood. It is not clear what year this is: some elements are contemporary, some are not. The film is black and white with a yellowish orange tint. And it's always windy.

1. EXT. BEACH—DAY (81 seconds)

An eleven-year-old boy, Eddie, is on a beach. He is seen from behind in an extreme long shot. He holds his arms out, Christ-like, facing the ocean. He falls straight back into the sand. He lies there a moment, then jumps back up. He repeats the action, falling backwards. He notices something near the water's edge. He pokes his foot at it then picks it up. He looks back towards the camera, self-consciously, then runs away.

2. INT. SUBWAY CAR—DAY (37 seconds)

Debris is blown across the train floor. The camera travels from the floor up to the face of Sonny, scruffy-looking, asleep on the train. The train rocks back and forth, then comes to an abrupt stop. Sonny falls off the seat, a rude awakening.

                         SONNY
          Shit.

Sonny gets up and exits.

3. EXT. SUBWAY PLATFORM—DAY (17 seconds)

[Opening credits: "Avenue X" (seen through windows of a passing subway train), "a film by Leslie McCleave"]

Sonny walks alone on the subway platform at the station (illustration 1).

1. Sonny (Brìan F. O'Byrne) returning from his night shift in Avenue X.
Copyright © 1993 by Mystery City Film.

4. EXT. ANOTHER SUBWAY PLATFORM—DAY (8 seconds)

In the distant background is a large parachute jump.
Sonny leaves the platform as trash is swirled by the wind.

5. EXT. DESERTED STREET—DAY (108 seconds)

Eddie is kicking a soccer ball against a corrugated
metal grate. The sound is very loud. Sonny walks
towards Eddie then in between the grate and Eddie but
doesn't acknowledge him. Eddie kicks the ball one more
time then turns to look towards Sonny. Sonny rounds a
corner. Eddie is still looking after Sonny. Hold on the
street corner. Sonny comes back around it. Eddie passes
the ball to Sonny. They exchange their special hand-
shake.

                    EDDIE
          Hey. Play to ten.

Eddie kicks the ball around a little then passes it to
Sonny.

                    SONNY
          Naw, not today. That was double
          shift I just finished.

                    EDDIE
          So you going home?

                    SONNY
          Yeh, soon.

                    EDDIE
          I have something for you.

                    SONNY
          What, a present? Or a bribe.

                    EDDIE
          I mean something to show you.

                    SONNY
               (concentrating on the ball)
          So, it will have to wait.

                    EDDIE
          Come now.

Eddie takes the soccer ball away from Sonny.

                    SONNY
          You can't disrupt a man from his
          routine.

Sonny takes the ball back.

                    EDDIE
          Oh come on.

                    SONNY
          Come by later on.

                    EDDIE
          You promise?

A group of four kids comes running down the boardwalk led by a ten-year-old girl, Lucille. The kids run between Sonny and Eddie and in doing so Lucille kicks the ball away from Eddie. The other kids go running in a pack after her.

Eddie starts to move off in the direction the kids have run.

                    EDDIE
                 (continuing)
          You promise?

                    SONNY
          Yeh. Promise.

                    EDDIE
          I gotta go get my ball.

Eddie runs off. Sonny walks in the same direction.

6. DOWN THE BOARDWALK. NEAR THE PARACHUTE JUMP—DAY (133 seconds)

Off screen: a calliope is heard. Eddie is running down the boardwalk. Dolly with him as he looks for the other kids. He jumps down off the boardwalk to an area with a derelict ride, the parachute jump. The other kids are

standing in front of a large metal fence, heavily graffi-
tied in different languages but clearly marked as a "keep
out" "danger" "no trespassing" kind of place.

                    EDDIE
             Where's my ball?

Marco mimes kicking a ball and makes an arcing motion
with his hand, indicating that the ball has gone over the
fence.

                    EDDIE
                  (continuing)
          Oh man.

They all look up at the parachute jump for a while
assessing the predicament.

                    ROB
                  (to Eddie)
          You're tallest.

                    EDDIE
             (irritated, he's heard that
                a million times)
          You're oldest.

                    MARCO
          It's your ball.

                    EDDIE
          It's the ONLY ball. Besides, you
          kicked it.

                    MARCO
          I didn't kick it.

Studying Scripts and Films

Marco points to Lucille.

> MARCO
> (continuing)
> She kicked it.

> EDDIE
> (to Lucille)
> Are you gonna go get it?

> LUCILLE
> (to Eddie)
> I'm not going over there.

> EDDIE
> You kicked it.

> LUCILLE
> So?

> EDDIE
> You have to.

> ROB
> Yeh, Lucille. Go get it.

> LUCILLE
> Fuck you.

> LUCINDA
> Ohhhh, I'm tellin'.

Lucille shoots Lucinda a quick no-nonsense glower then turns and walks along the perimeter of the fence. Eddie follows her.

                    EDDIE
Chicken. Chicken little . . .

                    LUCILLE
Shut up, Eddie.

                    EDDIE
You're aaffffrrrraaaiiidddd.

                    LUCILLE
Oh, like you're not.

                    EDDIE
              (looking up at the tower)
Of what? It's just some rusted
hunk of junk . . . (O.S.) Staller.

                    LUCILLE
I'm not stalling, I was gonna tell
you what happened, but if you
don't want to hear, that's OK with
me. It's your loss, man.

                    EDDIE
So what happened, chicken?

Lucille turns towards the kids.

                    LUCILLE
              (matter of fact)
Something bad.

                    MARCO
It was left over from aliens.

All three laugh at Marco.

                    ROB (to Marco)
Don't be stupid.

                    LUCILLE
Do you guys want to hear this or
not?

                    ROB (O.S.)
Well?

                    LUCILLE
OK, a long time ago the guy that
owned this place had this kid, right,
so the kid didn't like to go on rides.

                    EDDIE (O.S.)
              (to the other kids)
What a baby.

As Lucille talks, Eddie becomes more transfixed by the
story.

                    LUCILLE
So one night the dad came home
real drunk, and he shook the kid
and said 'Wake up—come on.
We're going on the ride. . . .'

Lucille's story quickly becomes indistinct. As the camera
dollies past her face through a hole in the fence, we hear
music and see a montage of the parachute jump.

                    LUCILLE
              (continuing)
"Oh, you wouldn't know. I've done
it a million times," and the boy says,

2. Eddie (Nickemil Concepcion) looks up at the abandoned parachute jump and starts to visualize what Lucille is saying in *Avenue X*. Copyright © 1993 by Mystery City Films

> LUCILLE *(cont'd)*
> "Oh I guess you're right" and he
> jumps off.

As we hear this conclusion of Lucille's story, we see Eddie staring upward (illustration 2).

7. EDDIE'S VISION (3 seconds)

Eddie's vision, in color, of a small boy in a nightshirt falling and falling through the air. The boy's face is both terrified and ecstatic. He seems to fall at Eddie's feet.

8. NEAR THE PARACHUTE JUMP—DAY (12 seconds)

LUCILLE
"BAM"

Eddie comes out of his reverie. There is no boy at his feet now. The other kids laugh at Eddie. Eddie rolls his eyes, ignoring Lucille—then walks off.

9. EXT./INT. PARACHUTE JUMP—DAY (61 seconds)

Eddie goes through a bent section of the fence. He walks bravely to the base of the tower. He can see the ball glowing in the dark. It is very dim inside. The ground is littered with broken glass and empty vials. Sitting in the back of the tower in the dark is a junkie, a woman, very old looking, though she's probably in her 20s. She has a baby's pacifier in her mouth. Eddie does not see her at first because it is too dark inside. But he startles when he reaches for the ball and suddenly happens upon her. She doesn't react to him. Eddie stares for a moment then grabs the ball and runs out of the jump.

10. EXT./INT. BOARDWALK BAR—DAY (56 seconds)

In the distant background is the parachute jump. The bar opens to the outside like a café so it's a partial interior that is open to the boardwalk. Sonny is sitting at the bar having a drink. All except him are old men and no two sit together. No one says anything for a while. Throughout the scene, an old song plays in the background.

BARTENDER
(to no one in particular)
Nice out today.

One of the patrons nods in agreement. Sonny looks out then finishes his drink.

SONNY

See ya.

BARTENDER

Yeh. Hasta mañana, Sonny.

Sonny walks out and onto the boardwalk. It's windy.

11. EXT. BOARDWALK—DAY (97 seconds)

3. *Avenue X:* Sonny on the boardwalk and on his way home. Copyright © 1993 by Mystery City Films.

Sonny is walking on the boardwalk (illustration 3). Garbage is swirled by the wind. There is no one else on the boardwalk. Out of the swirling garbage a shredded black plastic garbage bag blows up towards him and entangles itself around his leg. He shakes his leg to get it loose. It seems to have a mind of its own.

He keeps walking and shaking his leg. Panics a little; the more he tries to shake the bag loose, the more the bag winds itself around his leg. He ends up tripping over his other foot and falls on the boardwalk. The bag falls off.

He sees the bag lying on the boardwalk, harmless. Sonny laughs a little to himself. He looks around to see if anyone saw him fall. There is no one else around. He brushes the dirt off his hands and begins to get up. When he does, the wind picks up again and the bag blows towards him.

                    SONNY
          Stay.

The bag stays in one spot but flutters a little as if it could be picked up by the wind at any moment. The bag moves forward a few inches.

                    SONNY
                 (continuing)
          Stay. Stay.

The bag stops and flutters in one place. Sonny laughs a little.

He looks around self-consciously and then standing like an authoritative dog owner.

                    SONNY
                 (continuing)
          Come.

A nearby dog whimpers. The bag blows towards Sonny. Sonny laughs enjoying the game. The bag blows next to his leg and alongside it but doesn't grab him.

> SONNY
> (continuing)
> Heel, heel, heel.

The bag obeys and blows next to his leg, keeping step with him. Sonny takes a few steps down the boardwalk, the bag following. He looks down at it.

> SONNY
> (continuing)
> Piss off.

Sonny kicks the bag and continues on his way. He glances back at it. The bag is picked up by the wind and rushes towards his head. Sonny looks alarmed then turns and takes off walking rapidly down the boardwalk.

12. INT. HALLWAY OF BUILDING—DAY (92 seconds)

We can hear Spanish TV bleeding through the walls. Close on Eddie unwrapping something. Inside is a gun.

> ROB (O.S.)
> Eddie, wannta play some hall ball?

> EDDIE
> In a minute.

Eddie rewraps the gun and places it on a window sill. Rob comes down to the stairs above Eddie and kicks the ball down the stairs. Eddie kicks it back.

> EDDIE'S MOTHER (O.S.)
> Eddie, not in the hall!

They resume their playing. Sonny begins to go up the stairs, intercepts the ball, and heads it.

EDDIE

Hey.

SONNY
(imitating Eddie)

Hey.

EDDIE
(following after Sonny)

Where are you going?

SONNY

Going to sleep.

EDDIE

You wanna see that thing?

Off screen Rob continues to kick the ball around the
hallway.

SONNY

What thing? Oh no. Not now, OK?
I'm going to bed.

EDDIE

But you said . . .

SONNY

I know. I said later.

EDDIE

Yeah.

Eddie turns to go then turns back.

EDDIE
(continuing)

You sure?

NEIGHBOR (O.S.)
Get going.

The neighbor one flight up glares down from the land-
ing. She is in her 50s, a faded flower, and she holds a
small dog that looks as old as she is.

NEIGHBOR
(continuing)
Go play outside.

SONNY
Come on, Eddie, I've been working
all night. I'm shot.

EDDIE
Fine.

NEIGHBOR (O.S.)
It doesn't get kicked against your
door!

Sonny unlocks his door and goes inside.

13. INT. APARTMENT—DAY (50 seconds)

Sonny shuts the door. The sound of playing in the hall can
be heard inside the apartment. A few seconds later the
ball comes crashing against his door. A picture by the
door jumps a little on the wall.

The camera moves with Sonny through his room revealing his things. the apartment is larger than one would
expect but sparely furnished, a table and chairs, bed, sink,
and a large radiator. There are two large windows at the
end of the room. They are smudged with dirt. The walls

Studying Scripts and Films

4. Sonny in his rooms in Avenue X. Copyright © 1993 by Mystery City Films.

haven't been repainted in thirty years. Sonny feeds his fish (illustration 4) then begins to get ready for bed.

14. INT. HALLWAY—DAY (13 seconds)

Eddie is sitting on the stairs and holding the wrapped-up gun.

> ROB
> So watchya got?

> EDDIE
> Nothing.

The two boys walk towards the stairs.

                         ROB
              Just show me.

                         EDDIE
              Nyah.

The two start to go down some stairs.

15. INT. SONNY'S APT—DAY (22 seconds)

Sonny is finishing washing his face. He walks to a window and pulls down one of the shades, cutting out some of the light. Sonny kicks the radiator in a vain attempt to get the banging pipes to quiet down.

16. INT. BASEMENT BOILER ROOM—DAY (38 seconds)

The sound of the banging pipes is louder down here. The "ping" as Sonny kicks the radiator echoes down to the basement. Eddie unwraps the gun and shows it to Rob.

                         ROB
              Cool! Where'd you get it?

                         EDDIE
              Found it.

Eddie aims at Rob and pulls the trigger.

                         EDDIE
                      (continuing)
              Pow!

Eddie hands the gun to Rob.

ROB
(closely examining the gun)
It's full of seawater and shit.

Rob aims at Eddie. The gun goes off. Eddie falls back-
ward (seen briefly in slow motion).

17. INT./EXT. SONNY'S APARTMENT—DAY (21 seconds)

The sound of the gun is heard in Sonny's apartment, but it
doesn't sound that different from the banging of the pipes.

Sonny is pulling down the last window shade in his
apartment. As he reaches for it, a shredded black plastic garbage bag blows vertically past his window. He
watches for a moment then pulls the shade.

FADE TO BLACK

End credits (74 seconds)

[*Avenue X* is included in the videotape cinéBLAST!4, a collection of
short films that is available for purchase. To order, call 1-800-860-
8896 or access http://www.cinemaparallel.com. The videotape
cinéBLAST!4 may also be rented from Facets Multimedia. To rent, call
1-800-331-6197 or access http://www.facets.org.]

The Resurrection of Broncho Billy
A Cutting Continuity Script
by John Longenecker and William H. Phillips

FOR HIS SENIOR YEAR project at film school, producer JOHN LONGE-
NECKER formed what he called the Super Crew from talented film students he knew at the University of Southern California cinema
department to make a western short film that would star his friend
Johnny Crawford and that would win an Oscar. After *Broncho Billy*
won the 1970 Academy Award for best short subject, Longenecker
arranged for Universal Studios to release the film theatrically, and the
studio made 35 mm prints and distributed the short on a double bill
with its line-up of feature movies each week for more than two years in
theaters across the United States and Canada. *Broncho Billy* holds the
record as Universal's most financially successful live-action short film.

Each crew member contributed as story authors to *Broncho Billy*,
Trace Johnston adding the old-timer scene, Nick Castle the final ride
off into the sunset, John Longenecker the "cattle drive" through cars at
an intersection, the "shoot-out" with the man in a crosswalk, and other
scenes. Trace Johnston, who was set to direct, left film school after the
script was completed. James Rokos stepped in as director and later
has worked in production. John Carpenter (film editor and original
music) has gone on to compose music and to direct feature films including *Halloween, Escape from New York, The Thing,* and *Starman*. Nick
Castle (cameraman) has directed feature films including *The Last
Starfighter, Dennis the Menace,* and *Major Payne*. John Longenecker
works as a cinematographer and second-unit director.

The Resurrection of Broncho Billy is a twenty-one-minute film. It
was made at the USC in 1970 and stars Johnny Crawford and Kristin
Nelson. In the same year, it won the Academy Award for best live-action

short subject. (The film's title and credits list "Broncho" instead of "Bronco" as a tribute to Broncho Billy Anderson, who is considered the first cowboy movie star.)

THE RESURRECTION OF BRONCHO BILLY

A cutting continuity script by the film's cowriter and producer, John Longenecker, and William H. Phillips. Included are the running times of each section and scene and all the transitions between scenes other than cuts.

Opening credits (13 seconds):

The Resurrection of Broncho Billy
Story By
Nick Castle
John Carpenter
Trace Johnston
John Longenecker
James Rokos

An intertitle card (12 seconds):
Sky is his ceiling,
Grass is his bed,
A saddle is the pillow
For a cowboy's head;
Where the eagles scream
And the catamounts squall,
The cowboy's home
Is the best of all.

FADE-OUT, FADE-IN

1. INT. ATTIC BEDROOM—MORNING (61 seconds)

Cowboy movie posters on walls (illustration 5). Billy asleep. Off screen, someone knocks on door.

5. The first shot of *The Resurrection of Broncho Billy,* one of many posters for Western movies that line the walls of Billy's room. Courtesy of John Longenecker.

> WOMAN (O.S.)
> Dubrawski, it's 8:15. You'll be late
> for work.

Billy wakes, sits up in his bed, puts on his cowboy hat, and starts to put on his pants.

2. INT. BEDROOM—DAY (83 seconds)

Now in his pants and shirt, Billy looks at cowboy movie posters and finishes getting dressed, adjusts his hat, poses in mirror, picks something off his teeth, starts to leave, then tosses his cowboy hat onto the cattle horns affixed to the brass railing on the back of his bed.

DISSOLVE

3. EXT. BY GATE AND MAILBOX—MORNING (41 seconds)

As Billy looks into a mailbox, a woman who is sprinkling
a lawn with a hose approaches him.

> WOMAN
> Morning, Bill. Putting the rent in
> the mailbox?

> BILLY
> Morning, Mrs. Castle.

> MRS. CASTLE
> Two weeks overdue, you know.

> BILLY
> Well, I'm getting paid Thursday. I
> expect a raise . . .

> MRS. CASTLE
> (interrupting him)
> Honestly, I don't know how you
> get away going to work dressed
> like that. You oughtta dress decent
> like everybody else does.

Billy sighs and walks away. Mrs. Castle calls out after him.

> MRS. CASTLE
> (continuing)
> And spending all that money on the
> movies. That's ridiculous. You
> oughtta put some of that into paying
> your rent.

Billy continues to walk away.

The Resurrection of Broncho Billy

MRS. CASTLE
(continuing)
You oughtta be taking a course at
night school. Learning a decent
trade. Who does he think he is,
Buck Jones?

DISSOLVE

4. EXT. RESIDENTIAL STREET—MORNING (18 seconds)

Billy walks over the crest of a hill, tall trees on either
side. He kicks a pine cone.

5. EXT. NEAR A HOUSE—MORNING (13 seconds)

Billy approaches a house.

6. INT. LIVING ROOM OF MR. TUCKER'S HOUSE—
MORNING (135 seconds)

Billy enters.

WILD BILL
Good morning Billy.

BILLY
Morning Mr. Tucker. [In the film it
sounds like "Decker."]

WILD BILL
How are you?

BILLY
Ah . . . fine. Running a little bit
late this morning.

6. Billy about to be captivated yet again by the old-timer's Western tales. Courtesy of John Longenecker.

Billy sets down a newspaper on the table and sits down.

> WILD BILL
> Yeah, well that's better than not
> gettin' here at all.

Billy picks up a cup of coffee and chuckles (illustration 6). Dissolve to Western images.

> WILD BILL
> (continuing)
> There [sic] years later when I was
> a youngster they used to unload
> the cattle, and the horses, and the
> government mules, and the hogs,

WILD BILL *(cont'd)*
and sheep. Unload 'em there and
run 'em out of the north and south
divide because there was a law
come in there, thirty-six-hour law,
that they had to unload 'em at a
certain . . .

Dissolve to image of a bucking horse and rider.

WILD BILL
(continuing)
. . . No, I only rode one bronc. And
he started to buck, and I jumped off
him, and he . . . (chuckle) he run
into a stone fence and killed himself. But I've ridden a lot. I used to
ride every day.

Dissolve to other Western images.

WILD BILL
(continuing)
. . . You take a Colt .45 you know
and a .44 with a seven- and-a-half-
inch barrel . . . I had that Texas-
made double Colts. Even Poncho
Villa used that type of gun down
in Mexico . . .

Dissolve to other Western images.

WILD BILL
(continuing)
. . . You know Wild Bill Hickok
when he went to bed he always
put ah newspapers in front of the

WILD BILL *(cont'd)*
door. You see you don't have to
see a man to hit him. I'm not a
good shot because I never shot
enough, but if I wanta hit a fella
in back of me, if I heard him I
could hit him. See I have those
famous Schofields and also the
famous guns that I can shoot backwards as fast as I can forwards.
But a . . .

Dissolve to other Western images.

WILD BILL
(continuing)
. . . Ya see when he went into any
place . . . Where he made his mistake in Deadwood's where he went
in and sat down with these fellas
with his . . . not with his back to the
wall. Ya always set [sic] with . . .

Dissolve to close-up of Wild Bill.

WILD BILL
(continuing)
Jesse James was killed ya know in
1882.

BILLY
[Why] you were born while . . . it
was all . . .

WILD BILL
. . . I was born ten years later. But
ah I was born April 11, 1892. Jesse

WILD BILL *(cont'd)*
James was killed April the third
1882 at 1318 Lafayette in Saint Jo
Missouri by Bob Ford. Bob Ford
was killed by O'Kelly. O'Kelly was
killed by Joe Burnett. Joe Burnett
was killed by Bud Thurman. Bud
Thurman was killed by Big Jim
Cortwright. Big Jim Cortwright was
killed by Luke Short, and Luke
Short's the only one that died a nat-
ural death. He died south of
Wichita, Kansas in 1893. The rea-
son I know that is my name is
Tucker, and Bony Tucker disarmed
Luke Short.

Dissolve to Billy and Wild Bill.

BILLY
My watch doesn't seem to be
working.

Wild Bill takes the watch from Billy, winds it, then snaps
the cover shut as he says the following.

WILD BILL
One thing I told ya Billy, when I
gave ya this watch, you have to
wind it every once in a while.

7. EXT. CITY STREET—DAY (13 seconds)

Billy walks through cars moving slowly in traffic as we
hear the sound of a cattle drive: cowboys whistling and
yelling and cattle mooing and bleating.

8. EXT. YARD OF HARDWARE STORE—DAY (48 seconds)

From blackness a shed door is opened by a stock boy in a work apron who picks up and carries something from the shed to the side of a building. Billy hustles around the corner and into the yard.

> STOCK BOY
> Hey Billy, you wanna give me a hand here?

Billy rushes over to him and helps him carry a heavy bucket of something to the side of the building.

7. Inside a hardware store, Billy (Johnny Crawford) has finally made it to work; then his boss (Ray Montgomery) continues peeling an apple and gives Billy the silent treatment. Courtesy of John Longenecker.

STOCK BOY
(continuing)
The boss wants to see you. He's
not too happy about you showing
up late all the time.

Billy hesitates outside the building's door then puts a
toothpick in his mouth and looks resolute.

9. INT. HARDWARE STORE—DAY (43 seconds)

Billy stands in the back-lit doorway for a moment, then
enters with a swagger as though he were about to con-
front a bad guy, tossing the toothpick onto the floor. We
hear only his footsteps. As Billy reaches the cash register counter, the boss is peeling an apple and ignoring
Billy (illustration 7). Billy inches closer, rests his fore-
arms on the counter, and waits.

FADE-OUT

10. EXT. YARD OF HARDWARE STORE—DAY (49 seconds)

Billy opens a screen door at the side entrance of the
hardware store and leans up against the doorway looking out into the shed yard. He puts a toothpick in his
mouth. We hear a saloon piano playing in the background and horses and wagons going by.

STOCK BOY (O.S.)
Well, fired you again huh?

BILLY
(after a long pause)
Yup.

Billy starts to walk away.

STOCK BOY (O.S.)
Hey Broncho.

Billy turns, catches an apple that the stock boy tosses him, gestures a thanks, and walks away.

11. EXT. CROSSWALK OF CITY STREET—DAY (90 seconds)

Billy is on the sidewalk of a city street surrounded by tall office buildings. He watches a man dressed in a business suit and hat and carrying a briefcase on the other side of the street and walks parallel to him for a block. As they wait at opposite ends of a crosswalk, the DON'T WALK sign changes to WALK. With the man on one side and Billy on the other (illustration 8), they step off the

8. Billy looks as if he is about to have a showdown and shootout with a man on the opposite side of a downtown street corner. Courtesy of John Longenecker.

9. In the crosswalk, the man dressed in a suit looks at Billy and is concerned about his unusual crosswalk behavior. Courtesy of John Longenecker.

curb and into the crosswalk (illustration 9). It looks as if Billy is ready for a gunfight, but has no holster and no gun. They meet in the center of the crosswalk then pass by. The man reaches the far curb, looks back at Billy, puts on sunglasses, and walks away.

12. EXT. FRONT ENTRANCE OF A TAVERN—DAY (4 seconds)

Establishing shot of a tavern.

13. INT. DARK TAVERN—DAY (68 seconds)

A bartender behind the bar whistles quietly as he cleans a glass with a towel. At the far end of the room Billy enters. A customer in the foreground moves back into the barroom as Billy takes a seat at the bar. As he passes, the bar customer signals to the bartender for a beer then sits at the far end. The bartender serves a beer to the bar customer then moves back across from Billy.

                    BARTENDER
          What can I do for you, son?

                      BILLY
          Give me a shot of red eye.

Bartender stops wiping a glass.

                    BARTENDER
          Red eye? You got any ID?

Billy stands up.

            MAN AT OTHER END OF BAR
          Here you go, cowboy.

Man at other end of bar slides a partial mug of beer to Billy, who grabs its handle.

                    BARTENDER
          You're still gonna need some ID,
          son.

Billy stands up and tosses a coin onto the bar next to the beer mug leaving it spinning.

14. EXT. ALLEY IN BACK OF TAVERN—DAY (120 seconds)

Billy steps out of the back entrance of the tavern and into an alley running between tall buildings. Clock chimes echo through the alley. Billy walks slowly down the alley and hears the sound of jingling and footsteps, then a clicking sound. Two thugs appear suddenly behind Billy.

> FIRST MAN
> Hey cowboy, where's your horse?

> SECOND MAN
> Yeh, what are you, some kind of faggot?

> BILLY
> Don't call me a faggot.

The two men punch a prostrate Billy then run off with his watch and money, tossing the watch in the air from one to the other. Billy is still on the ground. He slowly revives, touches his lip, checks his now empty vest pocket, touches his lip again, then gets up slowly and, still recovering, walks down the alley. In the distance, he gives a kick to a bicycle leaning against the alley wall as he passes.

15. EXT. ALLEY ENTRANCE AND SIDEWALK—DAY (21 seconds)

Billy bursts out of the alley entrance and determinedly strides down the sidewalk with part of his shirt hanging out.

16. EXT. ORANGE JULIUS STAND—DAY (46 seconds)

A young woman behind the counter sets a drink on the counter. Billy picks it up and takes a sip (illustration 10). He speaks through glass window.

> BILLY
> I've just been in one hell of a fight.

10. Billy tries to impress the young woman at the Orange Julius stand about the "hell of a fight" he was recently in. (He got mugged.) Courtesy of John Longenecker.

The woman behind the counter bends over to speak out the opening below a window.

> WOMAN
> What?

Billy bends down so he can speak through the opening, too.

> BILLY
> I said, I've just been in one hell of a fight.

> WOMAN
> That'll be 26 cents.

> BILLY
> Oh.

He straightens up and starts looking through his clothes.

> BILLY
> (continuing)
> Just a minute.

He continues looking through his clothes, finds no money, and realizes it has been stolen by the two men in the alley. Billy grins sheepishly, leaves the drink on the counter, turns, and walks away. The young woman takes the drink back in and closes the sliding screen.

> DISSOLVE

17. EXT. CITY PARK—DAY (78 seconds)

Billy sits at the base of a tree. Someone comes up to him.

> WOMAN (O.S.)
> Hi.

Billy looks at her.

> WOMAN
> (continuing)
> Would you mind standing up?

Billy stands and looks at the woman.

> ARTIST
> (continuing)
> Thank you.

> BILLY
> What, what are you drawing?

11. In a park an artist (Kristin Nelson) sketches the cowboy (Johnny Crawford).
Courtesy of John Longenecker.

ARTIST
(smiling)
Oh, I was sketching you. And ah
you look so western and everything I thought I'd put you in a
western town (illustration 11).

She continues to sketch him.

BILLY
I should probably be wearing my
kerchief. It looks a lot more
western.

Almost simultaneously, he puts on a kerchief.

ARTIST

OK.

BILLY

Maybe I should tuck in my boots.
I mean my pants.

ARTIST

Sure. That's fine.

DISSOLVE

18. EXT. PARK PICNIC TABLES—DAY (162 seconds)

Billy and the artist sit on a park picnic table. The artist has
her sketch pad on her lap and is touching up her work.

BILLY

That's nice, but you know there
are a lot of things in there that
really aren't very authentic (illustration 12).

ARTIST

What do you mean?

BILLY

Well, I mean, you know, they're
all small, but ah they mean a lot
to . . . to cowboys. I mean like for
instance ah ya see ah his gun isn't
really low enough. John Wayne
always wears his gun low so that
he can hit it with his thumb.

ARTIST

Oh yeah?

12. Billy is critical of the details in the artist's sketch because they do not match what he has seen in Western movies. Courtesy of John Longenecker.

> BILLY
> If you've seen his films you could
> tell. And in fact, in all of them Gary
> Cooper always wore it low. He didn't
> wear it as low as John Wayne, but
> ah that's just one thing.

Billy points to the sketch with a twig he's holding.

> BILLY
> (continuing)
> And then this saddle over here, it
> doesn't have a flank strap. They
> gotta have a flank strap.

> ARTIST
> Flank strap?

BILLY

Flank strap. So that when they
rope a calf, it won't pull up the
back of the saddle.

ARTIST

How do you know so much about
horses? You have a horse?

Billy pauses to consider her question.

BILLY

Well, not all cowboys have their
own horses. Ya see, some cowboys
umm can't afford their own horses
and ah they just travel around to
different cow outfits with their . . .
their own saddles. Some don't even
have their own saddles.

ARTIST

Come on, cowboys have their own
horses.

BILLY

Well no, not all of them. Sure some
of them do. But ah I remember a
film with John Wayne where he
just walked around. He didn't
have his own horse or even his
own saddle. He had to borrow the
outfit's. They had ah they would
have a . . .

ARTIST

Listen, this is finished. Do you
like it?

BILLY

Well, if it's good enough for you,
it's good enough for me. But it could
be a lot more authentic. Because ah
well, you know, I imagine you
haven't done this sort of thing
before but if I just had my own hat
I could show you, ya know, that the
type of hat that they wore wasn't
quite like this. John Wayne always
wears a . . . a taller hat, you know.
That looks like a dude's hat. And
ah he had more of a curve to it. And
ah John Wayne he always wore a
different hat every single movie.
And it was always authentic. You
should pay attention to his hats . . .

ARTIST

Right . . .

BILLY

Because Cooper always had a good
hat. And sometimes it was you
know John Wayne always has the
same hat, every movie. But, you
know, it's a good hat. But Cooper's
hat was always different. I
remember in a film in Along Came
Jones . . .

ARTIST

Listen . . .

BILLY

He had the best hat. It was . . . it
was . . .

ARTIST

I'll see ya later. OK?

The artist gets down off the picnic table, and walks away leaving Billy sitting alone looking after her. He snaps the twig he's holding. We hear the sound of horse's hooves approaching fast. Billy leaps away from the table.

19. EXT. ROLLING HILLS—DAY (71 seconds)

The artist continues to walk away, now in an open western prairie and wearing nineteenth-century clothing. She turns back as the images turn from sepia to color.

Billy is a now a cowboy and rides over a rise on a horse toward the artist. He reins up his horse next to her. She

13. In his imagination, Billy gets a horse and the woman artist. Here, he even gets back the watch that the muggers stole from him. In the film this shot is in color. Courtesy of John Longenecker.

Studying Scripts and Films

14. The last shot of *The Resurrection of Broncho Billy*. In his fantasy, Billy and the artist ride away on the horse. They are seen in the distant background and on the right of the frame. In the film this shot is in color. Courtesy of John Longenecker.

reaches up and hands him his lost pocket watch (illustration 13). He puts it in his shirt pocket then takes her hand as she floats up onto the back of his horse.

They ride past a tree on the prairie, then across the crest of a hill, then across the crest of a hill farther away within the magic of a Western movie (illustration 14).

FADE-OUT

End credits (52 seconds)

[Those with further interest in the film or having questions about it can contact
Broncho Billy Pictures
P.O. Box 5155
Beverly Hills, CA 90210
Tel.: 310-276-8196
Web site: http://www.BronchoBilly.com/]

Scripts and Films
Goals and Means

EVERY DAY FILMMAKERS and videomakers—beginners and pros—start shooting a poorly conceived script that dooms the production. It need not be that way. Although writing and rewriting a script is time-consuming, a well-thought-out script is essential for making a film or video that entertains, expresses some of life's experiences, draws forth audiences' emotions, and in other ways involves viewers.

Whether storytellers are aware of it or not, the urge to tell stories is—as Robert Crichton said—natural, vital, intuitive, and ageless. From time to time, everyone feels this need. For some, though, it is more than a passing urge. For them, it can become a hobby; for others, a way of life and a means of supporting one's life. Whatever the case, it is a way to share with others a view of life's plenty. In its selection, invention, and arrangement of events, a story also imposes order on life and helps make sense of it.

Successful scriptwriters know that to make an effective film or video, even locally and inexpensively, is never easy, and that to win favorable reviews they must hold the viewers' attention. Successful scripts include some of the following: fascinating characters, suspense, surprise, humor, conflict, sexual attraction. For example, *That's What I Love about You* is an entertaining script: full of conflict and humor and with flashes of deeply felt emotion. *Rock of Hope* contains some complex characters, surprise, humor, and plenty of family conflicts.

The best short films also mirror life: they show people with goals and problems. *Rock of Hope* shows a family under considerable financial burdens and with a father who tries to cope with stress by drinking. *Avenue X* shows two characters with different goals and problems: Sonny is tired, though not too tired to get a drink before going home to rest; Eddie has no adult to share his dangerous discovery with. These and other short scripts tell stories that reflect life. And when we see the films made from these scripts, we believe we see life, or at least each writer's view of it.

Finally, the successful short film or video story involves the audience. To do so, the script, like the finished film or video, must capture the audience's interest in the opening minutes, and if it is to be a comedy, it must be funny early in the film. During the opening credits is not too soon.

It's important not to insult an audience's intelligence but to require them to watch carefully. If points in the story are obvious, viewers feel superior and distanced; they may feel offended. On the other hand, if the story is told subtly—as in *The Road* where a later scene mirrors the scene under the opening credits though without a romantic couple—audiences must stay alert, and in discovering significant details, they will take pleasure in their findings. They will stay involved. (More about obviousness and subtlety below.)

When you plan your script, a major concern should be your prospective audience. By considering this early, you will solve some problems that every writer faces between those first blank sheets of paper (or lonely, nagging cursor on the computer screen) and the final draft. As you write and rewrite, you must ask yourself repeatedly: Who is in my audience? What does it know? What does it not know? What can be left out? What needs to be shown in detail? You must understand the people in your audience if you are to write a script that will entertain them, mirror life, and involve them.

Once you know your audience, you should know how much to include—how obvious to be or how subtle.

A student once wrote about a married woman dissatisfied with an old station wagon she and her husband own and envious of another couple who own a better house and car. By the end of the script, however, the main character felt closer to her husband, and her situation did not look so bad after all. In the last scene, the couple drive off in their old station wagon with the license plate FMLYWGN, which is an effective, visual conclusion to the script. It's also subtle because, at story's end, readers have to figure out that the wife and husband are a family, not dissatisfied individuals. (Readers may also remember that this is the same car that the woman was unhappy with at the beginning of the story.)

Depending on the audience, the writer could have been more obvious or more subtle. An obvious ending that assumes an inattentive or unintelligent audience might have the woman comment to her husband, "Well, this old car doesn't look so bad after all." That's about as obvious as you can get. A more subtle approach might omit mention of the license plate altogether and end the script with the couple driving off in their old station wagon and expect readers to remember the wife's initial unhappiness with the car.

Whether aware of it or not, scriptwriters repeatedly choose how obvious to be, or how subtle. Scriptwriters should make those decisions after they consider how observant their audiences are likely to be.

If you write mainly for a small audience—and you will in most of your first short scripts—you should write for attentive and intelligent adults, an audience that resents zoom-ins to important objects, that gets the point the first time, or surely the second. Generally, readers of short scripts also do not want to read stories about life as it appears in popular movies or TV shows.

Visuals

Think about it for a moment; how many lines can you quote from movies? "Frankly, my dear, I don't give a damn" probably comes immediately to most minds. What other movie lines come to mind? Probably not many, even if you have seen many films, some of them repeatedly.

Now think about what images come to mind from films that moved you. You will have your own list, and if you love films, it will be long. What lingers in the memory is usually images, not words. As Jan Farrington says, "Movies, after all, are motion *pictures,* not moving words. . . . It's no accident that the screen's most memorable figures have been visual personalities, rather than 'speechmakers.' Bogart never had much to say, but his tight-lipped snarl and raised eyebrow spoke volumes. Gary Cooper made millions from his ability to convince audiences that he was speechless with shyness" (1984, 137–38).

To illustrate how much information images can convey, consider that in *Avenue X,* eight of its seventeen scenes are without dialogue; two have only one word; and another only six distinct words. In *The*

Resurrection of Broncho Billy nine of its nineteen scenes lack dialogue, and some scenes with dialogue—such as scene 10, where Billy admits to his coworker that he has been fired again—have only a few lines of dialogue. Below I'll describe and discuss briefly four of the most important scenes from *Broncho* that have little or no dialogue.

1. INT. ATTIC BEDROOM—MORNING (61 seconds)

> Cowboy movie posters on walls (illustration 5). Billy asleep. Off screen, someone knocks on door.
>
> WOMAN (O.S.)
> Dubrawski, it's 8:15. You'll be late for work.
>
> Billy wakes, sits up in his bed, puts on his cowboy hat, and starts to put on his pants.

The film begins by showing Billy's bedroom, which is full of posters for cowboy movies. Billy has attached a pair of cattle horns to the head of the bed and looped a lariat over a bedpost at the foot of the bed. He plays the cowboy role to such an extent that he takes his cowboy hat off the cattle horn and puts it on before he gets out of bed! His obsession with being a cowboy and with cowboy movies becomes evident quickly and visually. (The only spoken language in this scene is the off-screen voice of Billy's landlady calling out "Dubrawski, it's 8:15. You'll be late for work.")

2. INT. BEDROOM—DAY (83 seconds)

> Now in his pants and shirt, Billy looks at cowboy movie posters and finishes getting dressed, adjusts his hat, poses in mirror, picks something off his teeth, starts to leave, then tosses his cowboy hat onto the cattle horns affixed to the brass railing on the back of his bed.

The second scene, which is without spoken words, shows Billy immersed in a movie world, looking at cowboy movie posters as he finishes getting dressed as a cowboy. Because Billy leaves his cowboy hat in the room, the scene may also hint that he cannot fully live out his cowboy-movie life beyond his bedroom walls. Perhaps he leaves the hat because people, including his landlady, ridicule him if he wears it in town; perhaps his boss has told Billy not to wear that hat to work. Finally, the scene establishes the film's humorous mood when Billy tries to look tough as he poses in the mirror, then picks something off his front teeth and looks silly. He's no John Wayne.

9. INT. HARDWARE STORE—DAY (43 seconds)

> Billy stands in the back-lit doorway for a moment, then enters with a swagger as though he were about to confront a bad guy, tossing the toothpick onto the floor. We hear only his footsteps. As Billy reaches the cash register counter, the boss is peeling an apple and ignoring Billy (illustration 7). Billy inches closer, rests his forearms on the counter, and waits.

In this scene, Billy swaggers like John Wayne toward his silent boss in the hardware store; then Billy approaches him, slows down, and comes to a halt and waits at the counter, faced sideways toward his boss—who, still silent, is not even looking at Billy. We wait with Billy—and the scene ends without a word. There is no dialogue in this scene, only Billy's swagger, then waiting and suspense.

19. EXT. ROLLING HILLS—DAY (71 seconds)

> The artist continues to walk away, now in an open western prairie and wearing nineteenth-century clothing. She turns back as the images turn from sepia to color.

> Billy is a now a cowboy and rides over a rise on a horse toward the artist. He reins up his horse next to her.

She reaches up to hand him his lost pocket watch (illustration 13). He puts it in his shirt pocket then takes her hand as she floats up onto the back of his horse.

They ride past a tree on the prairie, then across the crest of a hill, then across the crest of a hill farther away within the magic of a Western movie (illustration 14).

The last scene is also without dialogue. Billy is on a horse and in a complete cowboy outfit—including a hat, a white one this time. He wins the young woman artist, and because this is a fantasy, he even gets back his stolen watch. In illustrations 13 and 14—the latter from the film's last shot—we also see rolling hills in the background. This setting is the only one situated outside of town and the only one in full color. Here the spaces are open and Billy is free, though he thrives in the country only in his imagination.

After studying scenes from *The Resurrection of Broncho Billy,* who can doubt the expressiveness and power of moving images? In seconds, we see if the story takes place in the past, present, or future, and where the action occurs.

Visuals reveal the characters' personalities to us. When the images are of the characters' faces, we see their feelings in ways words cannot describe. For instance, in illustration 7, Billy's boss does not look at Billy because he is annoyed with him for being late to work again, but the boss's expression conveys more than words ever could.

Visuals also establish a film's moods, such as in *The Road*, where the rain early in the story is appropriate to the story's initial melancholy mood. Visuals can even convey complex and subtle meanings, as in *Avenue X,* where the unnatural color and lonely settings hint at the isolation the characters experience.

All this, and more, visuals can convey quickly and efficiently. So powerful are visuals that you can tell a story without words, and some creators of short films who could include dialogue choose not to. If a film uses dialogue, typically not all scenes include it. So expressive are film visuals that you can watch a film that has dialogue and not listen to it and often still understand most of the film's meanings and moods. So important are visuals to film storytelling that most scriptwriting teachers require their students to write a script without dialogue, or at least scenes without dialogue. Some scriptwriting teachers do not allow students to write dialogue until well into the course, after they have proven they can convey a story without it. (For additional pointers on visuals, review the questions about settings and actions in the Script Checklists in chapter 10.)

Dialogue

Ambrose Bierce's definition of conversation in *The Devil's Dictionary* may be helpful. He described it as 'a fair for the display of the minor mental commodities, each exhibitor being too intent upon the arrangement of his own wares to observe those of his neighbor' (Stracznski 1984, 65).

Remember that a story on film or video need not have dialogue. It need not, but it usually does because dialogue—what is said and how—is a miracle of life and art.

Please review the following scene from *The Resurrection of Broncho Billy:*

16. EXT. ORANGE JULIUS STAND—DAY (46 seconds)

A young woman behind the counter sets a drink on the counter. Billy picks it up and takes a sip. He speaks through glass window.

BILLY

I've just been in one hell of a fight.

The woman behind the counter bends over to speak out the opening below a window.

WOMAN

What?

Billy bends down so he can speak through the opening, too.

BILLY
I said, I've just been in one hell of
a fight.

WOMAN
That'll be 26 cents.

BILLY
Oh.

He straightens up and starts looking through his clothes.

BILLY
(continuing)
Just a minute.

He continues looking through his clothes, finds no
money, and realizes it has been stolen by the two men
in the alley. Billy grins sheepishly, leaves the drink on
the counter, turns, and walks away. The young woman
takes the drink back in and closes the sliding screen.

It is a typical effective film scene in that it is short and has little dialogue (thirty words) yet reveals much. Billy unsuccessfully tries to
impress the woman with his tough-cowboy routine. He also orders
before checking whether he can pay for it. Part of Billy's character is conveyed visually—his sheepish look before he walks away, for example—
but part of it is conveyed by the dialogue, which is, I believe, exactly
right. Not a different word, not another word is needed. What Billy says
and, to a lesser extent, how he says it show his character.

A second example of effective dialogue is taken from a script and
film called *Lady's Man* by Dale Melgaard. In the excerpt reprinted
below, Morgan, the lady's man of the title, has come to visit a friend
(probably a former lover).

VERONICA
. . . Now tell me what's really on
your mind.

MORGAN

I don't know, love. I just felt like
your company, that's all.

VERONICA

Uh oh, a little trouble in paradise?
How are things with Aki?

MORGAN

Great . . . really.

VERONICA

Really?

MORGAN

Yeah . . .

VERONICA

Uh huh.

MORGAN

Look I'm not here to talk about
Aki.

VERONICA

OK, then tell me who died. You
look like you just came from a
funeral.

MORGAN

Ronnie, I'm fine, OK, I'm fine.
There's just a lot on my mind.

VERONICA

Morgan . . .

MORGAN
I feel good, I do . . . I feel great but
. . .

VERONICA
You feel great . . .

MORGAN
All right, tell me, why I'm so
depressed.

This dialogue shows both how difficult it is for Morgan to say what is on his mind and Veronica's closeness, skepticism, and concern. The lines of dialogue are short—and tentative. Note that twice Morgan cannot complete his thoughts (ellipses) and how at the end of the excerpt Morgan twice interrupts Veronica before he finally admits how he feels.

What lessons can be drawn from these quite different scripts? First, dialogue should be used only when it helps convey moods and information that visuals alone cannot communicate. In the scene from *The Resurrection of Broncho Billy,* we cannot know about Billy's boastfulness unless we hear him tell the young woman behind the counter about the fight. Conversely, where visuals alone do the job, dialogue should be omitted. In that same scene, when Billy discovers he has no money, leaves the drink, and walks away, no dialogue is needed. Knowing when not to use dialogue is one of the surest marks of a skillful scriptwriter; in fact, scriptwriters always prune dialogue as they rewrite.

Second, dialogue should reveal what the main characters are like, what they want, and the progress or lack of progress toward achieving such goals. In *Avenue X,* for example, Eddie tells Sonny he has something important to show him, but Sonny never gives him a chance to.

Third, what characters are like and what they want should often be expressed indirectly in dialogue, because what people say is often oblique, complicated, subtle. As the excerpt from *Lady's Man* illustrates, people often say one thing when they have something else on their mind; they seldom come right out and say what's important to them. In *Broncho Billy,* Billy does not tell the woman behind the counter that he is impressed with himself and she should also be impressed, because he's been in a fight (remember, he was mugged), although from his words we suspect that he is proud of himself and wants to impress her. Effective dialogue tells just enough to get us interested; then we viewers watch, listen, and figure things out for ourselves. That way we become involved with the characters and stay involved with them.

Fourth, dialogue should be concise. (Remember the scene from *Broncho Billy* has only thirty words of dialogue; two scenes in *Avenue X* have only one word, another only six distinct words; the excerpt from *Lady's Man* consists entirely of short sentences and fragments.) Though conversation off movie screens contains unnecessary words and insignificant pauses, film and video stories should not. The dialogue illustrated above seems natural yet less wordy and more revealing than actual conversation. Note also that effective dialogue contains only one point in each speech because audiences can grasp only so much at a time. What Raymond Hull explains about dialogue in plays applies to film and video dialogue as well: "A general rule is that each speech must convey only one idea. This is not a stylistic quibble; it is a practical necessity. Audiences cannot grasp complicated speeches. You must feed them information as a bird feeds its young, piece by piece, and you must allow time for the digestion of each piece" (1983, 106).

Finally, dialogue should be written with a minimum of directions to actors and directors, as in the excerpt from the screenplay for *Lady's Man:* the writer did not say how the performers should deliver their lines. There, as in most well-written scripts, no words of dialogue are underlined for emphasis, no "pause"s inserted, few ellipses used to indicate when performers should slow down or trail off in their delivery. Experienced writers know that it's usually unnecessary to indicate how lines should be said because what is spoken normally reveals how the lines should be said. Then, too, skillful actors can often deliver their lines more effectively than the writer imagined.

Scriptwriters sometimes indicate sound effects and music, though, as I have urged, beginning scriptwriters should generally concentrate on the visuals and dialogue. That's plenty to wrestle with in the early stages.

All five characteristics of effective dialogue are illustrated by scriptwriter John Hill, who shows how Robert Bolt could have written a scene from *Lawrence of Arabia* then how he wrote it:

Studying Scripts and Films

Here is what Bolt *didn't* write:

> TAFAS
>
> Drink some water now since you're not Arab and you'll need some but I won't since the desert's my home and I'm tougher.

> LAWRENCE
>
> That affects my pride personally and I'll show you and not drink until you do so you'll see I'm both different and serious and besides, I enjoy amusing myself for myself too. . . .

The way Bolt wrote it was:

> TAFAS
>
> Here you may drink, one cup.

> LAWRENCE
> (starts to, then notices)
>
> You do not drink?

> TAFAS
>
> No.

> LAWRENCE
>
> I will drink when you do. (puts water away)

> TAFAS
> (grunts and shrugs)
>
> I am Bedu. (11)

Bolt's version conveys moods and information that visuals alone could not; it reveals aspects of two important characters; the dialogue is indirect; it's concise; and it is written with no directions on how the lines should be said.

(For further pointers on dialogue, review the questions about dialogue in the Script Checklists in chapter 10.)

Stories

Settings, characters, structure, and meanings are the four major aspects over which the scriptwriter has control.

Beginning scriptwriters often give little thought to settings. If you see drafts of their work, even if they are divided into scenes, often they do not indicate where the scenes take place. If the locations are indicated, they are rarely described in detail. In their descriptions of settings, beginning scriptwriters normally present a fuzzy or blank picture.

Too bad, because a setting can do more than tell filmmakers or videomakers where to film the scene. Settings—especially the first time the living or work quarters of the main character are described—often reveal what a character is like. Settings sometimes also establish the mood of the scene. To illustrate, let's look at the description of the first setting of *Leon's Case* by Raymond Hartung. In that film, Leon Bernstein was a Vietnam War resister who mistakenly believes he is wanted by the FBI, so he dresses in various disguises.

1. INT. LEON'S APARTMENT—DAY

> Leon Bernstein is staring intently into a mirror as he carefully places a bushy, false mustache under his nose. Leon is a tall, skinny man of about thirty. His long hair, which is receding in the front, has been pulled back into a ponytail. He is dressed in the clerical garb of a Catholic priest. A recording of Bob Dylan's "Subterranean Homesick Blues" plays in the background. . . . [Leon] selects an appropriate hat from a hatrack that offers a variety of caps and helmets. The top of the dresser is cluttered

with manikin heads, beards, wigs, and other types of theatrical makeup. . . . His cramped basement apartment is something of a shrine for the social causes of the 1960s. The walls are covered with posters announcing the "MARCH OF DEATH," the "POOR PEOPLE'S CAMPAIGN" and other events. Pictures of Che, Malcolm X, King, and both dead Kennedys are prominently displayed. A Richard Nixon dartboard with the slogan "NIXON'S THE ONE" hangs on the bathroom door. Several darts perch from the famous nose and jowls. The few pieces of furniture in the apartment are distinctly of found-in-the-street vintage. Leon begins gathering together a large stack of papers that rest on top of his cinder block and plywood desk. The stack contains hundreds of pages, all sizes and colors. . . .

The scene shows Leon's attachment to the past, his modest lifestyle, his political views, his disguises, and his disorganization—all in the opening setting. From the descriptions—the darts in Nixon's nose and jowls, for example, and the theatrical disguises Leon hides behind—we know Leon is supposed to amuse us.

Like settings, clothes can also show viewers a character's personality and moods. In *Broncho Billy*, Billy's cowboy outfit allows him to more easily live out his fantasy of being a movie cowboy. Given Billy's obsession—he puts on his cowboy hat before he even gets out of bed—it's inconceivable that he would wear anything except a cowboy outfit: it's easier to get into a role if you look the part.

Most descriptions of settings in scripts are usually not as detailed as the opening description of *Leon's Case* and some scripts say little or nothing about clothing, but when you want to show someone's character, using setting and clothing is one of the quickest ways to do so. Occasionally, the setting or clothing will also help establish a mood and cue audiences about how they should react. Because so few original film or video scripts are published, for further examples you might play (and replay) the opening scenes of videotaped movies. You will find that many films quickly show the characteristic setting and clothing of the main character. (A short section on settings is also included in the Script Checklists in chapter 10.)

In films and videos we learn about characters mainly from their actions and words. Not that they explain themselves to us; they act, and interact. We see the characters; we figure them out.

Early in a short film, viewers need to know who the main characters are and what they want. Many beginning scriptwriters fail to show these two essentials, and readers flounder for page after page wondering what they missed. By way of contrast, in the opening scenes of *That's What I Love about You* we see that the two sisters are the main characters and what they want: for their mother to be well. Early in *Avenue X* we learn who the two main characters are and that they, too, have opposing goals. Once we know this, we can proceed without wondering whether we are on the right track.

After establishing the main characters and their goals, scriptwriters create obstacles that hinder those characters' progress. Remember in *That's What I Love about You,* Sylvia immediately has problems: her mother has told her to get Lisa up and to school (and we can tell that will be difficult); we also learn that Sylvia's mother is having an operation that day; and we can suspect that Sylvia is worried about it: after her mother kisses her perfunctorily, Sylvia hesitates then says good-bye rather than wish her mother good luck or express her concern. That's the first scene. Shakespeare often began his plays in the middle of a conversation shortly before something was about to happen or shortly after an important occurrence. He knew how to catch and keep the audience's attention.

When the central character seems true to life, wants something, yet runs into problems in getting it, we viewers stay interested. Conflict and problems attract and hold audiences. As Lajos Egri points out, "Since most of us play possum and hide our true selves from the world, we are interested in witnessing the things happening to those who are forced to reveal their true characters under the stress of conflict" (1960, 181).

Beginning scriptwriters sometimes include too many characters, and their stories lack focus and force. However, as *That's What I Love about You, Avenue X,* and *The Resurrection of Broncho Billy* all illustrate, most successful short films have one or two main characters. Because time is so limited in a short film and it takes time to develop characters, it is usually important to focus on only one or two. For a story to hold

Studying Scripts and Films

audience interest, we viewers must care about or at least be interested in the main characters. And unless the characters are treated satirically, they must seem so lifelike that we forget that the story is fictional.

Often first-time scriptwriters make the mistake of allowing the main character to achieve too much or change too drastically in a brief story time, but a short script should resolve little. For example, if the major character has problems at both work and home, it would be fantasyland to show success in both areas; that's hard to accept in the limited time span short scripts cover.

Remember, short scripts don't resolve very much. At the end of *That's What I Love about You*, although the sisters have come closer during this time of adversity, their personalities and conflicts (neatness vs. messiness, for example) will remain unchanged. By the end of *The Road*, four characters have gained something in their personal relationships though not the intimacy and family they had hoped for. By the close of *Rock of Hope*, it is unlikely the father will reform and family harmony be achieved. By the ending of *The Resurrection of Broncho Billy*, Billy is as much a dreamer as he ever was. (See the section on characterization in the Script Checklists in chapter 10.)

When you study short films, you will notice that nearly all have the main characters seeking a goal, coming up against problems in reach-

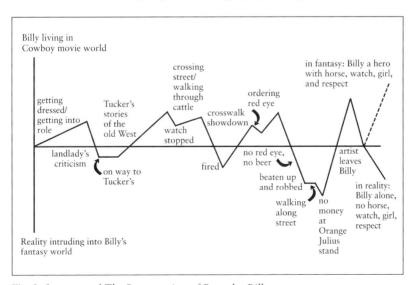

Fig. 2. Structure of *The Resurrection of Broncho Billy*

ing it, then either achieving the goal or not. The graph for *Broncho Billy* (fig. 2) illustrates this structure. Most effective scripts have the structure illustrated in figure 3.

character(s) seek(s) goal(s) ➞ conflicts/problems ➞ success/failure

Fig. 3. Basic structure of many short scripts.

Beginning scriptwriters often write excellent scenes yet come up short when they have completed their scripts. Structural flaws can ground their flight.

1. The main character(s) seek(s) a goal or goals. The script may have more than two main characters, which in a short script usually confuses the audience and lessens the story's impact. The central character(s) may not have a goal or may seem to have several unrelated goals. In effective scripts the major characters usually do not say what their goals are, but viewers should be able to figure them out quickly.
2. The character has problems or conflicts in reaching the goal. The central character may not face enough problems or conflicts in trying to reach the goal. Who would want to watch, for example, a twenty-five-minute film showing Billy getting cooperation from nearly everyone? Alternately, the script may have too many problems in a short story time (soap opera).
3. The character usually succeeds or fails to reach the goal. The story may veer off course and skid to a halt before an unrelated matter. Or, it may show us an ending that is inconsistent with the character or situations described earlier in the story; for instance, if Billy changed his personality and renounced his movie cowboy ways.

Often, we see briefly how the main character reacts to reaching or not reaching the goal. Many scripts end with that image. At the end of *Rock of Hope,* for instance, Pedro vows to change, but the two most aware characters are doubtful.

With so many ways for a story to go wrong, is it any wonder so many stories fail?

Many student scriptwriters begin their stories too soon, and readers must wait for the real story to begin. Experienced writers, on the other hand, often cut the beginnings of their early drafts. As Chekhov wisely wrote, "My own experience is that once a story has been written, one has to cross out the beginning and the end. It is there that we authors do most of our lying" (quoted in Bertagnolli and Rackham 1982, 55).

Effective short scripts do not try to cover a long period because that weakens dramatic effect. For example, when selected events from different years are shown in a short film, the story lacks unity and punch. The story times of *Avenue X* and *The Resurrection of Broncho Billy* cover no more than a few hours; the events of *That's What I Love about You* also take place on the same day: from a morning to late in an evening.

Scripts that work well have a change of mood from time to time. Regardless of what the dominant mood is—tension, melancholy, humor, whatever—lack of variety can be tedious, even in a short film. Usually in serious stories, such as *Rock of Hope,* at least one scene has humor, and in most effective humorous stories, some scenes have moments of seriousness, as in *That's What I Love about You* where Lisa reveals love for her sister.

Successful screenplays also leave out some actions. They exclude what is unimportant to the characters, structure, and meanings. *The Road* chose to only hint of Cecilia's relationship to the man we glimpse during the opening credits. To show their relationship in detail is unnecessary, even distracting—given the story's character and her present goals. What is important is that she yearns for a special man.

As scriptwriter William Goldman advises, you should always begin a scene as late into it as you can, as is illustrated in scene 10 of *Avenue X* where we see only the end of Sonny's trip to a bar. In that well-filmed and edited scene, that's enough to show the lack of warmth and community in the bar. Similarly, it's important to end a scene before it wears out its welcome. Walter Brown Newman, a professional writer, explains why it's best to keep only the essentials: "You tell the audience only what they need to know—no more. And as little of that as possible. I feel that a great deal of tension can be given to any scene, any character by keeping the information to a minimum. As Hitchcock said sometime ago, 'The one who tells you everything right away is a bore'" (Froug 1972, 66).

Contrary to what many beginning scriptwriters seem to believe, most effective short scripts avoid flashbacks. Of the scripts and films discussed extensively in this book, none uses flashbacks. Writers of short films should hesitate before using them. In the first place, they can confuse viewers. In the second place, flashbacks seem a little old-fashioned; current films usually don't use them. In the third place, flashbacks may show background material that contributes nothing significant to the story. For example, imagine that *The Road* had written in flashback scenes of Grandpa fishing with his son, Cecilia's father. That would disrupt the story and diffuse its focus on Cecilia.

Finally, an effective ending is crucial. Given the characters and their previous actions, the ending should make sense. An effective ending will not automatically assure the success of your script, but a weak one will sabotage it. As screenwriter Robert Towne points out, "An audience will forgive you almost anything at the *beginning* of a picture, but almost nothing at the end" (Brady 1982, 424). (See the section on structure in the Script Checklists in chapter 10.)

Every story has meanings. Its characters—their actions and interactions—show something about the way people are. The best stories show some of the complexity of human nature, such as conflicting emotions or opposing loyalties. *That's What I Love about You* shows two main characters who get on each other's nerves yet love each other. *The Road* shows lonely characters reaching out to others and forming tentative new friendships, though not the ones they sought at the beginning of the story. *Avenue X* shows how indifferent and dangerous a child's environment can be. As I interpret the story, *The Resurrection of Broncho Billy* is about an amusing and timeless situation, someone who lives in a fantasy world as much as possible and functions ineffectively in the everyday world. A story usually has several meanings, and different viewers will often see different ones and explain them differently. And sometimes audiences see meanings writers weren't aware of or didn't intend. That is one of the wonders of telling stories and learning what people see in them.

In well-written scripts, characters do not tell the audience what the story means (a sign the writer is uncertain of the story's effectiveness).

Instead the audiences discover the story's meanings. That way, viewers become more involved in the story and more impressed—by the story, by the scriptwriter, and, not insignificantly, by themselves. (See the section on meanings in the Script Checklists in chapter 10.)

Appendix to Part Two

Limitations and Possibilities of Short Scripts

For the short script, the key word is *limited*. Settings, characters, structure, and meanings—all must be limited.

Normally, a short film should not have many settings, otherwise the viewer sees none well and learns little from them. Many settings in a short film may also confuse the viewer and run up production time and costs.

The number of characters must be limited, too. Otherwise, in a twenty-or thirty-minute film, viewers get to know no one well and remain uninvolved, passive, at best vaguely interested spectators.

The structure of a short script should also be restricted: usually an effective short script has chronologically arranged scenes showing significant events in the life of the main character(s) during a few days or less.

Because meanings are determined by settings, characters, and structure, if those three components are limited, the meanings will be, too. If not, it can be a bewildering task to understand the point—let alone points, or meanings—of a short film.

Short scripts and short films are in some ways more restricted than feature scripts and films (fewer major characters and fewer story lines, for example); however, short scripts and films are not the impoverished cousins of features. The limitations of short films, especially their brief duration, make possible potential strengths. Because they are brief and can be seen repeatedly and with more concentration, short films can be more compressed, elliptical, symbolic, ambiguous—more demanding of their audiences but very rewarding, too.

As J. Stephen Hank wrote in a letter to me, knowledgeable "audiences tend to be more tolerant of, perhaps even more inclined to expect, ellipses and ambiguities in a short film . . . than in a longer one—a condition not unlike our willingness to accept ellipses and ambiguities in a poem that we would not expect in a novel. . . . I'm not sure that a short film is only an abbreviated version of a long film—it might also be denser, more ambiguous, more 'poetic.'"

Territories: Scriptwriters and Production Personnel

Before you write a script, it's a good idea to learn what writers usually put into a script and what the other filmmakers or videomakers usually contribute to the finished product. Table 1 illustrates the customary responsibilities of writers and filmmakers or videomakers—including director, cinematographer, performers, editor, and composer. Of course, in making a short film or video, one person often serves in more than one of these roles.

Table 1 The Writer's Territory	
The Writer's Territory	Territory of Production Personnel
Settings: where and when the action take place and what it's like there	*Casting and Performance:* persons, animals, or creatures selected to play the roles; behavior, gestures, tone of voice
Subjects: what the subjects do and say	
Structure: selection and arrangement of actions and dialogue (if any)	*Cinematography and Mise en Scène:* camera distances, angles, lenses, lighting, compositions, and so forth
Meanings stated in the story or more often implied by it: what the film explains about its subjects in general terms or more often shows about them	*Editing:* length and arrangement of shots; transitions between scenes*
	*Music and most sound effects**

*Occasionally, editing transitions, music, and sound effects that were indicated by the writer are followed by the production personnel.

Generally, if you write a script that others will finance and produce, it is best to stay largely in the writer's territory (table 1). Your role is to describe settings in which the characters act and speak. The writer also selects and arranges significant action and dialogue into a structure that shows meanings.

If you try to direct on paper—and many beginning scriptwriters seem to think they should—chances are you'll waste time, clog your script with roadblocks for your readers, and alienate your future director, who will promptly ignore most of your directions. You may also trigger resentment among the other people who will bring your script to life because they may think that you don't trust them and that you are telling them how to do their work.

If, on the other hand, you are certain you will direct your own script, put in those indications about camera, editing, music, and so forth. These will serve as notes to yourself when you sit in the director's chair. Even if you will direct your own script, it's usually better to include these technical notes in a late version of the script. Putting them in early may interfere with getting the story told. In the early drafts it is better to concentrate on settings, the characters' words and actions, structure, and meanings: with those alone, you'll have your hands full.

For brief descriptions of a variety of short films, including those cited in this chapter, see Films and Videos.

Part Three

Writing Scripts

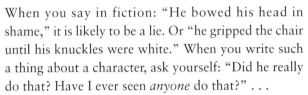

When you say in fiction: "He bowed his head in shame," it is likely to be a lie. Or "he gripped the chair until his knuckles were white." When you write such a thing about a character, ask yourself: "Did he really do that? Have I ever seen *anyone* do that?" . . .

When you have written a story and it has come back a few times and you sit there trying to write it over again and make it more impressive, do not try to think of better *words*, more griping words. Try to see the people better.

—BRENDA UELAND,
If You Want to Write, 136

Before You Begin

IN HER AUDIO-CASSETTE PROGRAM *Yes! You Can Write,* Elizabeth Neeld describes an art contest involving thirty-one student artists who had at their disposal different drawing materials and twenty-seven objects. Each artist was given the same amount of time to paint a still life with any combination of the objects. During the allotted time, each artist was observed by someone who wrote down what each artist did. After all the students had finished, independent judges evaluated their works.

The findings: the winning artists had picked up the most objects and explored them the longest. The winners, more often than those who did not win, changed their minds about which objects to include. They more often also changed the arrangement of the objects. They more often moved the objects to a different part of the room so that their paintings would have a different background. And they switched their media (watercolor to oil paint, for example) more often than others. In short, the winners spent much more of their allotted time making changes and considering the results.

I have seen the same results with writers. Those who remain open to possibilities, seek options, and try out many of them usually write more powerfully than those who quickly zero in on a story and stick with it, avoiding major surgery and making only cosmetic changes no matter how long they work on the story.

As you plan, write, and rewrite your script, do not settle on your story too soon. It will usually come into focus only as you experiment extensively: only as you plan, write, and rewrite again and again. Only then will you see more clearly what you have to show.

Sometimes beginning writers tell me that they write to express *themselves* and that they write for themselves. Writing is invaluable for expressing yourself, and it can be therapeutic. But writings for yourself should not be shown to others. What you share with others should be intended for others. Writers seeking audiences should remember that they are trying to involve prospective viewers. Film and video are not only self-expressive arts but also communal arts, so effective scriptwriters try to foresee the wants, strengths, and limitations of both the production staff and their audiences.

Because writing is so complex and personal, no writing technique will work for everyone all the time. Some of the suggestions in this part of the book will work for you, some won't. Remember: in writing, as in friendship and love, whatever works is good.

Planning 8

BEFORE YOU WRITE a first draft, even before you organize your material, be sure you know the main characters of your story well. To better understand the characters they plan to write about, some writers compose character biographies. They write about many of the main events that might have happened in their characters' lives from childhood up through the time in which their scripts take place. A short, but effective, variation of the character biography is to describe several of the character's most important experiences.

Even though little of this biography finds its way into the final version of the script, it helps some writers understand their characters more completely; it helps them spot vagueness, inconsistency, and improbability. This is another technique you need to try a few times to discover whether it works for you. The time to write character biographies might be before writing a discovery draft, treatment, or set of scene cards (all three are described below). Or perhaps you will prefer to write the biographies after the first draft or at another step. You should be on guard, however, not to spend too much energy writing character biographies. You don't want to tire of the characters before bringing their stories to life.

Nearly all experienced scriptwriters organize their material before they write their first drafts. They do so because in the long run it saves time. Try arranging the parts of your script before attempting the first draft, but remember the paths of writing have many byways, dead ends, and U-turns. Sometimes you cannot find the ending to your story until you finish a draft or two. Remember also you could spend too much creative energy on planning your script then run out of steam before completing the first draft.

It's a mistake for some writers to talk about their story before they write it because their enthusiasm and momentum slip away before the story is on paper. I say "some writers" because, again, writers work differently. Ray Hartung told me that after he completes a preliminary outline, he likes to get someone to listen as he describes each scene. This procedure helps him see problems with the story. It also lets him see how his listener responds, and it gives him a sense of proportion (for example, if a scene is too long). This procedure works for him, and it may work for you, but you should stay on guard against telling others your plans in detail before you write your script, or you may never write it. Some writers subconsciously avoid the hard work of writing by talking so much about what they plan to write they lack time or energy to write!

Organize then, but not to the point of exhaustion, before you launch into your first draft. Three ways to organize your stories are discovery drafts, treatments, and scene cards.

One way to start to find the story you want to portray is to write one or more discovery drafts of it. To do so, write your story as quickly as you can. As in focused freewriting (see chapter 1), write rapidly without judging what you write. As you write, do not worry about format, punctuation, spelling, and word choice. Do not worry about anything except the brief story of the main characters, and as quickly as you can, tell where each scene takes place and who does what, who says what. If you write this draft on a computer, try turning off the monitor, or turning it down, so you are not distracted by what you see on the screen as you write. While writing a discovery draft, do not stop and allow your mind to gag the creator of your writing and shove your internalized critic onto center stage.

When you finish this rough draft, instead of reading it, put it aside for a day or two. When you look at it in the fresh light of another day, you may see a promising beginning; the story may kick and cry for attention. If not, you may want to try a second discovery draft.

If one of your discovery drafts twitches with life, you should reread it carefully then weigh it against the following questions: Are any scenes impractical to film? Do any scenes require expensive makeup or costuming? Do they require special effects beyond reason? Do the scenes require many locations or expensive sets and props? Do any scenes make excessive demands on the performers available for the production? If you answer yes to any of these questions, revise your draft in light of the resources you have available.

Read your draft aloud. Are there too many characters? What is the main character's goal? Do we learn of it early in the story? What blocks his progress toward that goal? What helps progress toward it? Can any scenes be dropped? Do any scenes need to be added? Can any be shortened? Can scenes be placed elsewhere in the story with better results? What is the story showing in general about people's motives and behavior?

If you dislike any answers to these questions, revise your draft. After that, if you are relatively satisfied with the results, skip for now the next chapter—on writing the first draft—and read the chapter on rewriting, chapter 10. If, however, your discovery drafts are stillborn, try one or both of the following approaches.

A treatment is a summary of the story written in paragraph form, often with occasional snatches of dialogue. Unlike a script, it includes only major scenes and characters.

Some scriptwriters write a treatment or part of one before doing the first draft. It should always be written in the present tense. After you have written and revised your treatment, read it aloud then perhaps have someone else read it to you while you visualize it. At this stage, you should be asking questions about your story: Is any action impractical to film? Does your planned story require extensive makeup or elaborate costuming? Does your story require special effects beyond the budget? Does your story require many locations or expensive sets and props? Are any actions too demanding of the performers available to you? If so, revise as you consider the resources you have available.

Now ask these questions of your treatment: Do the main characters get lost in a crowd of characters? What are the main characters' goal(s)? Do we learn it early in the story? What blocks their progress toward that goal? What helps their progress toward it? Can any actions be omitted or shortened? Can actions be placed elsewhere in the story for a better effect? What is the story relating? Rewrite as necessary.

After you start to tire or lose perspective, put the treatment aside and do something completely different; then return to it when you are alert and energetic. Rewrite, take a break, rewrite, take a break . . .

When you are satisfied with the treatment, you may make scene cards (as described below), or you may divide your treatment into d write a first draft. If you write a treatment, keep in mind that make changes between it and the final version of the screen- it is natural. Don't worry.

Another way to organize a story is to write a description of each scene on a card, then revise some cards, add some, delete others, and rearrange the remaining ones. (In a way, you are editing the story before it is written and filmed.) If you have written a useful discovery draft or treatment, you will probably want to base your scene cards on that.

Let each card represent one scene, that is, an uninterrupted action in one location. On each card describe concisely the setting (place and time), characters, and action, and give snatches of dialogue if they come to you at this point and you don't want to chance losing them. (See fig. 4.)

---

27. INT. LISA'S HOUSE—NIGHT

Surprise birthday party. Picture-taking of
Marsha with husband and daughter. Jillian
heard singing "Happy Birthday" melody with
the words:

"Happy Birthday to you.
Happy Birthday to you.
You look like a monkey
And you act like one, too."

FADE-OUT

Fig. 4. Sample scene card describing the last scene of *And You Act Like One, Too,* which was written and directed by Susan Seidelman

If your story has related groups of scenes—usually called sequences —you may want to write each sequence in a different color of pencil or pen, or use different colored cards.

As you work with the scene cards, you need not write the descriptions of scenes in the order they will appear in the finished script. And if you have trouble getting a scene to come out right, don't allow yourself to become bogged down in it. Move on to other scenes; then return to the troublesome ones. Chances are, you will then know better how to describe them.

After you have finished describing as many scenes as you can, apply the same questions that you did for the discovery drafts and treatments and make needed changes. At this point, number the cards in pencil, and try pinning them on a wall or laying them out on a large table. Look again at your set of cards and ask the same questions as those applied before.

You might also try making up a second set of cards: on each one draw the main action of a scene. Put the sketch for the first scene on a bulletin board or on the floor, and under that card place the card describing the setting, characters, and major action of the scene. Continue arranging matched pairs of cards in this way until you have your story spread out before you. (Or, if you prefer, make up just one set of scene cards: on each put a drawing and a brief description of the scene.) Next, look at and read your rough cut and see where the story works, where it does not.

By organizing the visuals and descriptions of scenes in this way, you may notice, for example, that your main character disappears for too long during part of the story, or you may see that one scene has too many characters to be effective. (This combination of drawing and description is like a storyboard, which is a drawing and short description of each shot of a planned film or video story. Most beginning scriptwriters, however, do better to write scenes, not describe shots, and leave storyboards to directors who like to use them.)

Whether you use scene cards or a combination of cards describing and depicting each scene, try shifting a few cards around and rereading the results. If you are dissatisfied with the new story, you can go back to your original arrangement; however, if the new one seems better, renumber the cards or put letters on them. You should probably read and arrange the cards on different days. When you are fairly certain about the number, content, and arrangement of the scenes, you are ready to write a first draft. But as you do so, remember that your story is on cards, not in marble, and you will probably want to make changes.

Most scriptwriters like using scene cards (so do fiction writers and dramatists), because the cards help them structure their stories effectively before they begin writing.

If you plan to base your script on a particular person and suspect that person may not appreciate what you plan, or if you plan to use material that others have written, you should read the next section. Otherwise, you are probably ready to turn to the following chapter and read about writing that first draft, or—if you have written a satisfactory discovery draft—you may skip the next chapter for now and move on to the chapter on rewriting.

Because your script may be made public, you should be aware of certain laws of libel and copyright. I don't mean to alarm you. Only rarely does a script present legal problems, but because yours could, you should understand the following points before you write a script for publication or performance.

Because I have not studied law, I can offer only general guidelines. If you think you may need legal counsel about a controversial or touchy subject that you plan to go public with, contact an attorney with expertise in libel law. Similarly, if you are uncertain about copyrighted material that you plan to use in a script that will be produced and shown publicly, see an attorney who specializes in copyright law.

If you base a character closely on a living person—as I have urged you to do—you should consider whether that person and others will recognize the source for your character and take offense at your representation. If so, you could face legal pressures, even a libel suit, especially if the person believes that he or she is recognizable and suffers a damaged reputation because the character you created and made public commits illegal acts or engages in antisocial or generally offensive behavior.

In one instance, a woman claimed that a prostitute character in a man's novel was based on her, and she sued him. A court ruled that the similarities between the person and character were "insufficient to establish that the publication was of and concerning the plaintiff." The writer won. Sometimes writers lose. Win or lose, such cases are time-consuming, expensive, and nerve-racking. And they have become more commonplace in recent years. A 1987 trial and settlement between a psychiatrist and some of the people who made (and promoted) the feature film *The Bell Jar* provided another warning to authors to use care in drawing unattractive characters based on real-life people.

In the example of the woman who sued the novelist, the lawyers for the novelist and publisher argued that if the woman's suit "were successful, writers would be forced to create unrealistic characters and publishers would have to delete any similarities between fictional and real people." This argument supports the view that writers should draw on people to infuse vitality into their characters. The trick is to draw on people but not too often or too faithfully on a person who might bring a lawsuit or in other ways attempt to create misery.

Copyright matters are also complicated (various issues have not been tested in the courts, and much of the application of U.S. copyright law to particular instances remains uncertain). As a writer, however, you do not want to get bogged down in a legal swamp. But be aware that if your work is published or performed publicly, you must be careful about whatever previously written or performed material you use.

You are free to quote from or paraphrase materials that were published before 1978 but never copyrighted or whose copyright has expired, though you are expected to acknowledge your sources. Most writing, music, and film copyrighted before 1920 are no longer protected by copyright laws in the United States and are in the public domain.

As a writer you may normally also use selections from copyrighted works—including poems, song lyrics, stories, films, music—but if your script is produced, someone will need a clearance from the current copyright holder, who may ask to be paid a permission fee. Be aware, too, that a song or other music may be in the public domain but a particular recording of it may be copyrighted and thus cannot be used without permission in a film or video to be shown for profit.

By custom, if not law, writers rarely seek permission for materials they incorporate into writing for educational courses, and they often do not seek clearance for material incorporated into works that are published or performed locally for nonprofit, though they should always acknowledge their sources (otherwise they are guilty of plagiarism). If you seek a large audience or income from your scripts, or both, you should get permission from the copyright holder(s), or you chance a lawsuit for copyright infringement—or at least the threat of a suit. As a writer you have better things to do. Such as write.

Remember the benefits of relaxing after intense concentration and work. After planning your script but before launching into the first or later draft, you should probably take a long, diverting break.

Writing

ONCE YOU HAVE WRITTEN a discovery draft, or treatment, or scene cards, or all three—or have begun to organize your material by an alternative method—you are ready to write the first draft. There is no one way to go about it.

Writers work under different self-imposed conditions. Paul Engle informs us that the "German poet Schiller used to keep rotting apples under the lid of his desk because their smell helped him write" (Bertagnolli and Rackham 1982, 53). William Goldman, a scriptwriter, says that while writing the screenplay for *A Bridge Too Far*, which takes place during World War II, he played records of military music, and while working on *The Great Waldo Pepper*, which is set in the 1920s, he played pop tunes of the period.

Other writers work under other conditions of their own choosing:

> Among the writers I have met, one habitually worked lying down in the dark, in a trailer with its windows painted black, dictating into a tape recorder. Another, when he wanted to think about a new novel, got on a bus to a destination about four hours away— it didn't matter where. When he arrived, he boarded another bus and rode back; by the time he got home, he would have the novel all plotted out. Another thought about a novel for three months, then sat down in a specially designed cubicle, smaller than a telephone booth, and typed furiously for thirty hours straight. When he came out, the novel was done. (Knight 1981, 10)

Terrence McDonnell, a television scriptwriter, describes yet other writers with unconventional procedures:

I like to work in a place that has high cathedral ceilings. Psychologically it makes me feel my creativity is not constrained. I think all creative people use things like this. I have a friend who will only type on yellow paper. Another writes in the nude, obviously not at the studio. Another puts on old clothes and doesn't bathe or shave until he finishes. It sounds strange, but it works for them. Subconsciously, perhaps, it helps them to have no illusions about themselves and enables them to go for the truth of the scene or the pain of the characters more easily. Whatever it takes, let it work for you. (Miller 1984, 53–54)

In writing, perhaps especially in writing the first draft, whatever circumstances work for you are good.

One circumstance, however, is necessary for all writers: time set aside to work without distractions and interruptions. (I don't believe I have ever met or heard of anyone who liked to write a first draft with distractions and interruptions.) Without that clear stretch of road ahead, few writers get under way. Once under way, however, how they move forward is up to them.

You have written journal entries and done writing exercises and have found a promising source for a script. You have studied the screenplays and films in part 2. By this time, you have organized the story you plan to write and are in your favorite writing space at a propitious time. It's time to write the first draft of your script, but—"your hands are shaky and your knees are weak," and it's not from being in love. What has gone wrong? Nothing. It's normal, in fact beneficial, to be nervous before a performance because nervousness can stimulate creativity. Accept it without becoming preoccupied with it and begin writing. Don't wait for this feeling to go away. Don't talk about it. Just begin writing, and you will get caught up in the writing and forget the nervousness.

In writing the first draft, try beginning each scene on a new page. If you later decide to rearrange or drop scenes, it's easy to do and the results are not messy. Until your final draft, double-space everything so you'll have room for revisions.

As you write the first draft, be sure to indicate the setting, general time, major action, and dialogue for each scene, but you need not number the scenes.

Generally, in descriptions you should write short, simple sentences—and only a few at a spurt. As the film *The Screenplay* points out, "too much detail freezes the imagination" of anyone reading or producing a script.

In the first draft, rarely tell what a character is thinking or remembering or feeling. Often those processes cannot be shown on screen unless you use images to represent what is on a character's mind or have much narration, and usually you should do neither.

If you plan to direct your script, don't get sidetracked in the first draft by cinematography, editing, and sound, though you may want to include occasional brief descriptions of important sounds and music. During the first draft, don't worry about grammar, spelling, and punctuation. Don't worry about a lot of things. For most people, being self-critical while writing doesn't work. Often television and movies depict writers typing furiously, ripping a sheet from the typewriter then trying again, repeating this process over and over in frustration. Don't imitate television or the movies. This is a dramatic scene, but it is about the worst way to write, because the writers try to write and rewrite at the same time. For nearly all writers, that's disastrous. Write; later rewrite.

As you do the first draft and new material comes to mind, write it down. Later, when you reread and rewrite the script, if the new material does not fit in after all, you can cut it and store it in your journal or notebook. It's better to write when new material occurs to you and cut during the rewriting stage than to disregard new material and struggle later to create it.

If you don't know how to write a particular scene, skip it for now. Professional scriptwriter Ray Hartung told me that if the trouble persists, your mind may be trying to tell you that there's a major problem with the story. If you feel like writing scenes out of order, that is OK, too, though you should do so on separate sheets of paper that can be inserted later into your script.

If the creative fires smolder or die, don't despair. Do something else. Insights and surges of creativity often occur after an intense effort followed by relaxation. You can achieve only so much during a writing session, so don't try to force the process, or you may get writer's block.

Damon Knight explains how writers need to put their unconscious (or what he calls the "silent mind") to work, then check back with it from time to time, but not too often, and not too urgently:

> If the unconscious isn't ready, don't push. If you do, you are like a chess player who keeps telling his partner what moves to make. If that goes on long enough, of course your partner is going to say, "Well, play by yourself, then." And there you are, making all the moves by yourself. (Serves you right.)
>
> To be productive, the unconscious needs a lot of stimulating input—odd facts or fancies to knock together, insights, specimens, interesting data of all kinds. . . .
>
> Critics talk about "the well of inspiration," and they say that the well sometimes runs dry. What this means, in my opinion, is either that the author is feeling the lack of stimulating input, or that she has not given her unconscious time enough to think about the problem. Trying to force it is a mistake. (1981, 28–29)

Some people believe that nonverbal activity is especially effective for stimulating writing. One of my students said that riding on her bicycle nearly always helped her figure out what she needed to write. Dorothea Brande advises writers who want to recharge their creative batteries to "amuse yourself in wordless ways. Instead of going to a theater, hear a symphony orchestra, or go by yourself to a museum; go alone for long walks, or ride by yourself on a bus-top. . . . Books, the theater, and talking pictures should be very rarely indulged in when you have any piece of writing to finish" (1981, 133–34). If you read, Brande cautions, read material unlike what you are trying to write. Good advice for many; perhaps it applies to you.

Remember, too, that most of the first draft probably will need much more work. It usually does. As often happens when we take on a large and complicated task, we make errors and unwise decisions. It's OK. No mistakes, no progress. Just don't get bogged down in the parts that don't seem to be coming out well.

If you cannot finish the first draft in one sitting, try stopping at a moment of high tension, stop maybe in the middle of a sentence. That may sound like torture, or at least strange. But many writers find it easier to resume writing if they had stopped in midsentence. At least they have a sentence to finish.

People restart their writing in different ways. Peter Elbow advises writers to read some of their previous best writing aloud. "This gives you the actual psycho-muscular feeling for what it was like to put juice into words. By reawakening this memory/ feeling, you can more easily get into that gear again. Reading over your own good work is particularly useful when you are having a hard time getting warmed up—perhaps after a long period of nonwriting" (1981, 371). Some writers start a writing session by recopying the last few pages of what they wrote in their last session. For them, this process builds steam: it allows them to review where they have been and to move to new territory. Still others write quickly for ten or so minutes about whatever comes to mind (freewriting), then return to where they left off their last writing session and resume writing. The new writing may not dovetail neatly with the old, but the joint can be repaired later.

Some writers will read none of the first draft until a day or two after they have finished it: that way they can see it more objectively and start weeding, pruning, planting, and transplanting with a surer hand.

Many writers say the first draft takes sweat or blood, or both. Some authors believe that they cannot have sex and write well in the same day. Writing, to them, seems that demanding. In *Annie Hall*, the character who is a writer says after having made love, "There goes another novel." For many, after the first draft is on paper or a computer disk, the hardest, most exhausting part is done. It's a natural resting point.

Rewriting 10

EVENTUALLY, YOU SHOULD try nearly all the techniques for revising scripts that are explained in this chapter. But for any one script don't feel obligated to use them all; that could be overwhelming.

If you have trouble getting a scene to work, try drawing what you have in mind. Even if rough, your drawing may help you see what should be happening in the scene. Drawing and painting can help scriptwriters, as they can fiction writers. "I know a good many fiction writers who paint, not because they're any good at painting, but because it helps their writing. It forces them to look at things. Fiction writing is very seldom a matter of saying things; it is a matter of showing things" (O'Connor 1961, 93).

Once you have finished the first draft of your script or have it nearly finished, you should read it aloud. Do as Samuel Butler did and whenever possible read aloud to someone else. "If Molière ever did read to her [his housemaid], it was because the mere act of reading aloud put his work before him in a new light and, by constraining his attention to every line, made him judge it more rigorously. I always intend to read, and generally do read, what I write aloud to someone; any one almost will do, but he should not be so clever that I am afraid of him. I feel weak places at once when I read aloud where I thought, as long as I read to myself only, that the passage was all right" (1918, 109). As you read your script aloud, visualize what is happening in each scene and perhaps make notes on the copy, but do not interrupt your reading for long. Immediately after reading the script aloud, revise it.

To see if the story is complete, clear, and filmable, you may also find it useful to read aloud everything but the dialogue and directions for delivering it.

Next, put the script aside for at least a day. Then, have someone else read it aloud. As the other person reads your script, follow along on another copy and take notes on what might need revision.

After the script has been read aloud and rewritten, try writing a one-paragraph summary of the story—not the story you think you told, but the story you wrote. In one paragraph—no more—describe the essential characters and actions. Write and rewrite this paragraph. The summary should be shorter than your treatment (if you wrote one) and should describe the story of your first draft.

After you finish the paragraph, consider the following questions:

1. Is the story true to life and free from the influence of television and popular movies?
2. What is the main goal of the major character(s)? Do we learn of it early in the story?
3. What events help the major character(s) advance toward the main goal? What prevents progress toward it?
4. What does your story show about human motives and behavior?

If you don't like the answers you come up with, revise the script at once. Put the parts you cut into your journal for possible future use. The paragraph summary may help you see the main aspects of your story—characterization, structure, meanings—so that you can rewrite the script and improve it.

Making a list of possibilities is another technique you might try, especially if you think your script too short or parts of it underdeveloped. This technique helps you consider alternatives. After you have reread your paragraph summary, quickly jot brief answers for each for these questions: What other problems might the main character(s) face while pursuing the goal? How would the main character(s) and others react to those new problems? Let yourself go: quickly put down on your list the wild and silly as well as the reasoned and reasonable. Some other time, look at the outcome from this storm of thoughts. Has anything useful washed up?

You may also want to try this strategy: reread each scene, not necessarily in the order they occur in the script. As you do so, quickly jot what additional events might happen in the scene, or what actions might take place instead of the ones in the scene. Write quickly; do not judge. Another day, look at your notes and decide if you want to follow up on any. These are notes to yourself, most of which you will not use, but from tempests sometimes wash up treasures.

As you reread and rewrite your script, check for other aspects. For example, on a card or sheet of paper make a short list of what you hope to show in your script. With that card or sheet of paper in hand, reread each scene out of order. As you reread each scene, check your list of points. Does each scene show at least one? If not, omit the scene, or cut part of it, or add to it. (In using this technique, you may discover something else to add to your list, rather than cut a scene or part of it.) As you rewrite your script, make sure that you never show *and* tell; just show. For example, look at the following:

                              BOB
            How can you stand living with her?

    Raphael [ignores the question,] turns away from him,
    and starts unloading the car trunk.

The phrase in brackets is unnecessary, because readers and viewers can see that Raphael ignores the question. To point it out is wasteful and may be seen as insulting.

If you review the scripts in part 2, notice that the descriptions of actions are concise, and they include few "ing" verb forms (e.g., preferably "Sonny takes a few steps down the boardwalk, the bag following," not "Sonny is taking a few steps down the boardwalk, the bag following"). Make sure, too, that you wrote your script in the present tense. Your script presents actions that when filmed seem to happen now.

If you choose the right nouns and verbs, you'll need few adjectives and adverbs. Instead of writing "An angry Rosentene runs quickly from the room," you might write "Rosentene storms from the room." And as much as possible eliminate overused, worn-out phrases, such as "sad but true": they are like the canned music we ignore in public buildings.

Another way to tighten up descriptions is to eliminate phrases such as "we see" and "we hear." As Richard Walter writes, "The stuff in the wide margins—description, action, business—is information intended to be communicated visually. That within the narrower margins—for the most part dialogue—is to be communicated via the sound track. For writers to specify 'we see' or 'we hear,' therefore, is simply redundant. In a properly formatted script it ought to be clear precisely which is which" (1988, 137).

In descriptions of settings and actions, make sure you have put in only significant details. If you mention an object, it should be important to the story. (Remember the photograph of the old man and younger man in *The Road*.) If you describe an object, make sure what you describe about it is important to the story. For example, don't write "a red ball" when its color is unimportant; write "a ball."

Similarly, check to see that you have not described the characters' physical appearance in detail. If your script is produced, the performers will probably not match the looks you have in mind anyway. You should also usually avoid giving characters similar-sounding names, for example, Fred and Ned, or Jane and June. Why chance confusing readers and audiences?

One other point about descriptions: include in them only what can be seen in the finished film or video. In the following three examples, the bracketed phrases indicate information that the film's images could not convey:

Ted comes in [from a trip to the massage parlor]

[Eight days later, on a Thursday]

Marilyn [realizes that Bob has lost control and] rushes toward the wrestling men.

If you must include the information in brackets, work it into the dialogue.

As you rewrite, also try to remember that in nonprofessional films and videos certain actions are difficult to present convincingly. For example, it would be difficult to show a person having a heart attack and make viewers believe it. Better to show how people react to this crisis. Remember, less is often more: sometimes it's better to leave certain actions to the viewer's imagination.

William Goldman advises scriptwriters to begin each scene as late into the action as possible: "You always attack a movie scene as *late* as you possibly can. You always come into the scene at the *last* possible moment, which is why when you see a scene in a movie where a person is a teacher, for instance, the scene always begins with the teacher saying, 'Well, class . . .' and the bell rings. And then you get into another scene because it's very dull watching a man talk to people in a room" (Brady 1982, 88–89). See whether you can cut the beginning of any of your scenes.

While you are in the cutting mood, note whether your script contains superfluous directions to future directors. A student once wrote a scene that included descriptions of the sources of the light and shadows, the sources of the sounds, two angled shots, and a close-up. Those directions got in the way of the story, and most were not needed. Setting, action, and dialogue are necessary—usually nothing more.

Have you minimized parenthetical remarks instructing performers on how to deliver lines? Have you unnecessarily underlined parts of the dialogue to indicate what the actors should stress? Have you used ellipses for trailing off in speech or for pauses when they weren't needed? Richard Walter says, "In keeping with their naïve and futile mania not merely to write but to direct the entire film from their typewriters, writers often wish to compel actors to pause or hesitate when they deem appropriate. Yet in context, effectively honed dialogue conveys such pauses naturally. Crafty dialogue invites the actor to discover the emotion on his own. He might even invent some nuance superior to that which the writer intended" (1988, 97). Nearly all directions to actors, underlining, and ellipses should be cut: readers, directors, and actors rarely need them.

How much rewriting you will need to do is impossible to gauge in advance but probably much more than you thought when you began. You should work on your rewrites while you are strong and alert—and do so on different days. Remember that most successful writers spend much longer on rewriting than on writing. When you are sure you have done all you can to improve the script, set it aside for a few more days, then reread it, check your summary, check your lists, review the other pointers in this chapter. If you wrote a treatment or scene cards, perhaps update them and reread them, too. Chances are, you will see still other ways to improve the script. Don't be surprised if you do, and don't be impatient to finish. "Talent [I read somewhere] is long patience."

Script Checklists

After you have written two drafts or three or four, you may want to use the following questions to help you see if your script needs more revision. Don't be surprised, though, if you don't use all these questions. If you try to apply all of them to your script, you may feel overwhelmed.

The most important questions you should ask of your script are about its sources, because poor sources doom a script from birth. Is the script yours: does it show your experience, your perspective, your language (or those of someone you know extremely well)? If not, whom are you imitating? A favorite writer? A friend? A television show? Some popular movie?

If your script passes the test on sources, examine it further by applying some of the following questions:

Settings

1. Is the setting of each scene indicated?
2. Have you avoided settings you know only from movies and television shows?
3. Do you have so many settings that it would be difficult or costly to film or videotape your story?
4. For a setting described in detail, is all the detail significant to the story? If so, is the detail easy to capture on film or video?
5. Does the setting of each scene show something about the character who occupies it?
6. Do some settings, such as a dimly lighted room, contribute to the mood of the scene?
7. Do the clothes ever reveal a character's personality or mood?

8. Do clothes help establish a scene's mood and clue in audiences about how they should respond?

Characters

1. What is the main character's goal? Can readers see what it is early in the script? What blocks his progress toward that goal?
2. Are there too many characters, given the short length of the script?
3. Are the characters' names easy to remember and distinct from each other?
4. Review your script and underline the actions of your main character. Are they believable?
5. Do you sometimes indicate a character's reactions to an action (such as a heart attack), rather than show the action?
6. Take a colored pencil or pen and underline all the dialogue of your main character; then reread that dialogue aloud, including noises that the character makes. Does the dialogue sound true to life and to the character's personality? Does it show the character you intend?
7. Take a pencil or pen of a color different from the color used above and repeat the process for all important characters.
8. Are silences used to establish a mood, such as tenseness? Are silences used to convey uncertainty? To suggest that something is difficult to express in words? All three options are available to writers.
9. Do the characters interrupt each other? Finish each other's lines? Sometimes trail off without completing thoughts? Effective dialogue often has these real-life traits.
10. Are there incomplete sentences? Colloquial words? Contractions (such as "don't" for "do not")? Speech and dialogue may have all three.
11. If a character uses slang, is it used only occasionally to suggest the flavor of the slang? To suggest a dialect do you use only occasional words and phrases rather than many phonetic spellings? Do not try to re-create real speech in its entirety. That's not good enough for your viewers. Be selective.

12. Are moods and meanings hinted at and left unsaid? Usually they should be.

13. Which lines can be interpreted in two or more ways and need to have a direction in parentheses to indicate how the performer should say them? As much as possible, write dialogue so that directions are unnecessary because directors and performers will ignore most of them anyway.

14. Are any sentences or passages too long? Good dialogue is more concise than conversations we hear in life.

15. Do some scenes contain much dialogue but little movement? If so and if that dialogue is necessary, consider having the characters do something as they communicate with each other. What they do should fit into the scene and be in character; it should not be busywork.

16. Does each speech convey only one idea or point?

17. Does the dialogue supply information unobtrusively and without insulting the audience's intelligence?

18. Does the dialogue sometimes reveal indirectly what the characters are like and what they want? Remember in life, people are often oblique, not forthright.

19. Do characters who know each other well use first names only occasionally? Remember in dialogue, people who know each other well rarely use each other's first name. They just talk to each other.

20. Perhaps most importantly, can dialogue be cut because the visuals of the scene convey the meanings and moods already?

Structure

1. Does the story's opening motivate the reader or viewer to learn the rest of the story?

2. Should some of the opening be cut? Or does the story begin too soon: do we need more preparation for the story to come?

3. Does the story cover a week's time or less? (Generally, that's a good idea for short scripts.)

4. If flashbacks are used, are they employed only after the reader has become caught up in the story? Do they show important

comparisons or contrasts between past and present situations? If not, why are flashbacks used rather than a chronological version of the story?

5. Given the characters and the story's meanings, can any scenes be omitted?
6. Given the characters and meanings, can any scenes be shortened?
7. Do any scenes need to be more fully developed?
8. Can scenes be rearranged in a different order to create a better result?
9. Is there more than one mood in the story?
10. Review a script from part 2; then review figure 2. Next, make a graph of the major actions of the main character in your script. Where does the main character make or not make progress toward his major goal?
11. Is the ending appropriate? Is it indeterminate about what might happen next, or does it leave viewers with a sense of completeness? Given the story and characters, is the ending justified?

Meanings

Review your story's settings, characters, and structure.

1. What does your story show in general about human behavior?
2. Does the story show complexity in human nature (such as conflicting emotions or contradictory allegiances)?
3. Does the story sometimes explain what is already evident to observant viewers? If so, cut the explanations.

Guidelines for Formatting

Before you show your scripts to others, you should use an acceptable format. I say *an* acceptable format because different organizations and guidebooks specify slightly different formats. An acceptable format applied consistently will help experienced readers understand your script with a minimum of interference; it will also demonstrate that you know your business.

As you become more experienced in writing scripts, you will want to write all drafts in an acceptable format. For most beginners, however, to write a script and format it at the same time is overwhelming. Beginning scriptwriters should concentrate on settings, characters, structure, and meanings; rewrite and revise thoroughly; then put the script into an appropriate format.

Until you are directed otherwise, the format described below and illustrated in figure 5 will serve the needs of whoever directs your story. For each scene in your script do the following: first, set your typewriter or word processor so that the left and right margins are about 1 1/2 inches wide (people producing your script will have room to write in notes). As you type your script do not trespass into those margins.

At the left margin, put the scene number. (Not all scriptwriters number the scenes, but scene numbers are useful in group readings and discussions and in film production.) Then in capital letters write: "INT." or "EXT." plus the setting, and if necessary for clarity, "—DAY" or "—NIGHT" or the part of the twenty-four-hour period.

After skipping two lines and beginning against the left margin, write a concise description of the scene's setting (optional) and first action. You should write this in brief sentences, typed and single-spaced. When a character's name is first introduced in the description, some scriptwriters capitalize the entire name.

Skip two lines then write the name of the character (typed in capital letters and centered in the page). When absolutely necessary, in parentheses and centered below the character's name, describe how performers should deliver the lines.

On the line below the character's name and indented 1 1/4 inches from the left margin and running three inches, single-space the dialogue.

The name of the next speaking character appears two lines below, spaced as above. Any additional brief description of significant action in the scene should be written as it was at the beginning of a scene.

When a character speaks, then someone does something, then the same character speaks again, use a "(continuing)" under the character's name, as is illustrated in figure 5. And when you must break a character's speech between pages, repeat the character's name atop the second page followed by "(cont'd)," as in "CECILIA (cont'd)."

11. INT. RESTROOM OF A CLUB—NIGHT

A group of women wait in line to use one of the stalls. Gloria stands next to a lady.

> LADY
> (to Gloria)
> I feel too old to be here.

> GLORIA
> Are you twenty something?

> LADY
> I'm thirty something, and a mother of four.

> GLORIA
> Wow, you look great!

> LADY
> My ass is getting big

The woman looks at herself in the mirror.

> LADY
> (continuing)
> At work I sit down on my butt all day. Eight, nine, sometimes even twelve hours a day.

> GLORIA
> My ass is getting big, too.

> LADY
> I feel fat.

> GLORIA
> You're not fat

> LADY
> I'm a single mother. My kids wear me down. I don't have time for myself anymore.

> GLORIA
> Raising four kids must be hard.

> LADY
> That's why I'm out tonight. To get away from my kids. I divorced my husband three years ago. He didn't care much about the kids. And me, well, that's another story.

Fig. 5. Master scene format (a scene from *Unexpected Circumstance* by Marlene Warda)

Technical indications, such as sounds and camera directions, should be kept to a minimum, but when you include them, they should be written in capital letters. Transitions between scenes—fade-out, dissolve, wipe—are written in capital letters aligned with the right margin at the conclusion of a scene. Do not put "CUT TO" at the conclusion of scenes—as many beginning writers do and even some scriptwriting books advise. Readers should understand that one scene cuts to the next unless otherwise indicated.

For the next four situations, you will find slightly different advice in different sources, but the formats below work well.

If you alternate from one scene to another ("intercut"), do it this way:

INTERCUT SEQUENCE:

    1. beginning of the first scene . . . conclusion of the scene
    2. beginning of the second scene . . . end of the scene
    3. third scene, same location as the first scene, etc.

END INTERCUT SEQUENCE

You may indicate a montage—a series of shots, usually combined by dissolves, used to present a condensation of events—this way:

MONTAGE SEQUENCE:

    1. [first scene]
    2. [second scene]
    3. [third scene], etc.

END MONTAGE SEQUENCE

To indicate a dream or fantasy, label the beginning and end of the dream or fantasy so that you do not confuse your readers:

[scene number, setting, time] (DREAM) or (FANTASY) . . .
(END OF DREAM) or (END OF FANTASY)

If you use a dream or fantasy, say so. Don't make your readers guess, as beginning scriptwriters seem to like to do; you'll probably confuse your readers and be disappointed that they did not fathom what you mean.

Indicate flashbacks similarly:

[scene number, setting, time] (FLASHBACK) . . .
(END OF FLASHBACK)

By using the format described above and illustrated in figure 5, you will find that a standard page of screenplay with dialogue will take about one minute of screen time.

The last step in putting your script into its going-out clothes is to make up the title page. No rigid rules dictate its contents and format. You may type the title in capital letters and place it within quotation marks in the middle of a blank sheet. On the next line or two type "A Screenplay [or Videoplay] by [your name]." Do not follow the title page with a page listing the cast of characters: that's used only for plays.

Now, at last, you are ready for your first cast and for your first, modest efforts at directing.

Reading Aloud in a Group, Discussing, and Revising

> If you feel that you must read your script to a relative or friend, do so. But don't ask him to comment on it. He may know infinitely less than you do and is likely to do more harm than good. He does not have the qualifications needed to give expert advice, and you will be forcing him into an unfortunate and painful position.
>
> If you must read your work to someone, ask that person to tell you the moment he begins to feel tired or bored. (Egri 1960, 178)

After writing, rewriting, and formatting a script, many writers rush it to relatives or friends—and usually come away from them more convinced than ever that they have written the world's first flawless script! Other writers have relatives or friends who insist that the script is worthless. Unfortunately, rare are the relatives and friends who are useful critics. Rare are people who can read a script carefully and tell you precisely their reasoned responses as well as any useful suggestions for improving it.

Instead of showing your script to relatives or friends, have a small group study it. Next, have each person read aloud the dialogue of one character, and one person read aloud the descriptions of the settings and action. Afterward, ask the readers to explain their responses to the script. You may want to tape-record the reading and discussion. The best group members not only read their parts with appropriate feeling but also have background in reading scripts. The ideal group member also has the elusive but essential characteristic—sound judgment.

Writers need skilled readers of their drafts because writers are rarely astute critics of their own work. They are too involved—too enthusiastic or too depressed about their work to see it clearly and judge it fairly. Often readers point out something about a script that the writer was unaware of. That's why writers should listen to readers. As the German philosopher Nietzsche said, "The author must keep his mouth shut when his work starts to speak."

After the reading and discussion have run their course, the writer should collect the notes, revise the script as soon as possible, then take a breather. The writer should then read the script aloud again and revise further.

Readers give incomplete and often contradictory responses. Normally, later readings yield new understanding of the script, so keep rereading your script as long as you are not sick of it, even after you finish considering others' responses. If you continue, however, to reread and rewrite your script after you tire of it, you will do more harm than good. You may even do major damage. When you start to tire, stop working on the script. Look at it again only after you are rested.

If you have read and written few scripts, please be especially careful to heed the following advice: in group discussion of characters, writers should avoid using "I," "me," "mine," "we," "us," and "our(s)." When discussing characters, the group readers should avoid "you" and "your." In group discussions about characters, use "she," or "her(s)," or "he," or "his," or "they," or "their(s)." By doing so, you are discussing the fictional script, the most useful focus for group discussions.

If you plan group readings and discussions, you may want to consult the following checklists, which contain more detailed and systematic suggestions than given so far.

The Writer

1. The writer should supply a copy of the completed and revised

script to each group member a day or more before the group reads the script aloud and discusses it.

2. As the group reads the script aloud, the writer should make notes on a copy: points to ask the readers after the reading, corrections of the script, phrases that seem difficult to read smoothly or don't sound right, what readers read instead of what is written, how listeners responded to different parts of the script, and so forth.

3. Writers should not tell the group the source of the script or their intentions or meanings. If you have brought your child up well, it should be able to speak clearly for itself.

4. Do not tell your group what outside readers said about your writing. Don't say, for example, "I showed this script to three friends, and they said it was wonderful" and, by implication, "why are you so dense?" Again the writing should speak for itself.

5. After the group has given extensive feedback, the writer should ask questions about parts of the script that still seem to need work. Be sure to take notes on how the group responds to your questions.

To summarize: in group discussions the writer should only listen, take notes, and ask questions.

The Readers

1. Each reader should read the script at least twice and mark questions, comments, and corrections on it before the group reads the script aloud and discusses it.

2. After the script has been read aloud, group members should give many specific and descriptive reactions to it. What did the writing make you think and feel? Why did it do so?

3. Give evaluations and advice only if the writer asks you to. Sweeping and vague judgments—such as "It's great," or "I don't like it"—are of little help to the writer and may even be harmful. Much more useful to writers are readers' specific and descriptive reactions. Tell the writer, for example, "The first scene makes me think of _____." "This character shows that _____." "The script suggests _____ because _____." To give specific and descriptive reactions, you

might fill in the blanks of this sentence: "This _____ makes me feel/remember/wonder/think _____ because _____." You might also ask the writer what if something else happened in the script (or did not happen). A good way to keep your comments specific and descriptive is to reread important passages aloud and tell the writer what they make you feel/ remember/wonder/think.

After the group has given its specific and descriptive reactions and has given the writer chances to question the group, you might ask the writer if he or she wants evaluation and advice. (If not, that's OK: usually specific and descriptive reactions are much more useful to writers than evaluation and advice anyway.) If the writer wants evaluation, you could say one of the following: "This _____ is effective because _____," or "this _____ is ineffective because _____." Advice could take this form: "What if you tried this: _____?"

4. Generally, give your positive reactions first. Even an experienced and confident writer may become defensive if faced with an opening barrage of negative comments.

5. Each group member should write notes on the draft to give to the writer after the discussion. As someone makes a particularly useful observation or asks an important question, someone else in the group should write it on the draft.

6. When asked at the right time and in a supportive way, questions are as useful as responses. Sometimes more so.

7. Members of the group should not spend time arguing with each other. Instead, concentrate on giving the writer responses and the reasons for those responses. Don't point out a disagreement with another member of the group; tell your reactions to the writer, not to another group member. For example, it's negative and argumentative to say the following to a fellow group member: "That scene does not show _____." Better to say something to the writer like this: "To me this scene shows _____." Later, the writer can decide which responses are useful.

8. The writer's autobiography should not be a topic for discussion. Nearly all effective short scripts will contain some fact, some fiction, but it's unimportant which parts are which. Do not

assume that a character is based on the writer. Might be. Might not. Besides, in terms of the script, what does it matter?

9. If one person begins to dominate the group discussion, other group members should talk more often.

10. If the discussion comes to a halt, wait awhile. If the discussion still lags, the writer might ask questions about parts of the script or ask group members to reread a scene that does not seem right and respond to it.

11. It's not worth group time and energy to discuss spelling, punctuation, and capitalization. They should be corrected on the copy of the draft that will be returned to the writer after the discussion.

To summarize: In group discussions the emphasis should be on the writing, not the writer, and the feedback should be specific, descriptive, and sometimes positive.

The following are sample marginal notes that suggest what the writers might omit or rewrite, and they let the writer know what the reader notices (and in some cases appreciates).

Omit (in brackets)

1. How does this fit into the script? OR
   Is this important to the script? OR
   Can you prune any of this?

2. Omit this and let us figure this out later?

3. We can tell already. OR
   We can well imagine this. OR
   We need not be told.

4. Omit? We have already seen this.

5. Just show us, and let readers make the judgment. ("He was a little less diplomatic.")

6. The "descriptions" judge too often. Let the reader discover and decide.

7. Do you want a pause here? (a comma or ellipses that need not be included unless the writer wants actors to pause briefly in the reading)

8. Too obviously a message (and brackets around a group of generalized sentences that interrupt the story for too long or seem wrong for the situation)
9. This scene begins slowly: no tension or humor or sex (earlier scenes established that the script is partly about sexual relations). Cut the beginning and begin later in the scene?
10. Redundant:
extended [out],
reverted [back],
sat [down],
also . . . [as well],
swayed [gently] in a light breeze,
herded [like cattle] onto the bus,
thought [to herself],
a [brief] moment, and countless others.
11. Would he? (for a character speaking out loud to himself, which most people rarely do)
12. Where else? (for "His heart began to pound [in his chest].")

Rewrite, or Rewrite and Add Details

13. Show us. Don't tell us. ("She was not at all happy about this new friendship"; "He was quickly losing his temper")
14. Is this what you mean? (for a word that doesn't fit in)
15. Show us at least some of this. ("The pain had taken her to her breaking point.")
16. Use a verb?
had a feeling ➝ thought or felt
had a tendency ➝ tended
makes an agreement ➝ agrees
17. Vague word ("magnificent")
18. Would they? (for something out of character that two characters did)
19. I cannot see this. (a fuzzy description).
20. How so? You need to be more specific. (someone runs "making plenty of noise")

21. In what sense? I cannot see this clearly. (for "a broken iron gate" Does it sag? Does it drag? Is it hard to open and close? Is it warped? Is it rusted, too? Peeling?)
22. The script *tells* us so much there's little for readers to discover and thereby become involved with.

Reactions to Story Developments

23. Because she did _____ in the second scene, I was surprised to see her do _____ here.
24. I've been expecting this to happen since the first scene when ___.
25. I laughed out loud here.
26. I smiled as I read this.
27. It doesn't make sense to me that he would _____ here because of _____.
28. I've been curious about what he would do if she _____.

Praise or Reassurance

29. Effective short reply.
30. This creates curiosity. (A scene ends, "Wade stands and smiles as he views the contents" but only later in the script do readers learn what the contents were.)
31. He doesn't answer her question. (This shows the writer I noticed this.)
32. Helpful (or vivid) detail

    "When she looked at him, she had to take one step back to get a clear, full view." This *shows* she's small and he's big.

    [during a meal] "Edward asked [a question] through his napkin"
33. I can see this. (for a particularly vivid description or vivid details)
34. Imaginative comparison ("When the vehicle was unloaded, it rested like an insect carcass under a huge mango tree"—from a script set in a Latin American country)

Let me remind you that not all these strategies will work for you. In writing, try out many of these suggestions, and use those that you like. There is no formula for planning, writing, and rewriting.

Epilogue
Reaching Listeners and Viewers

A SCRIPT UNREAD or unproduced is like a musical score or architectural drawings sitting in a drawer. Scripts, scores, and architectural drawings are made for production. Writing the script may have been challenging and satisfying, but it was written for others to see and hear what you had in mind, and you should work to see your best short scripts come to light. They may do so in two ways: public readings and video or film productions and showings.

For many scriptwriters, a public reading of their script helps them see how audiences react to their story and helps them understand their script's strengths and weaknesses. A program of short scripts by several writers will draw a larger audience than a program of scripts by one writer, because most writers have friends and family who will attend. With the help of fellow writers—or, even better, people with training in oral interpretation or acting—you can put together a program of short scripts. Keep the program under an hour; otherwise, it's hard to hold your audience's attention. Before the reading have at least one rehearsal.

In reading a script, each participant should read aloud one character's lines, and one person should read the descriptions of the settings and actions, though not the occasional, brief directions to performers on how to deliver lines. If you have more parts than readers, you can double up on minor parts, but try to avoid having the same person reading consecutive roles.

If possible, the author should be in the audience listening to what parts of the script read well, what parts do not. The author should also take notes about how the audience responds and about parts of the script that may need rewriting.

After the reading, you can eavesdrop on the audience to learn its reactions. Or you may invite it to remain and ask questions and make comments on the scripts. Or you may ask members of the audience to fill out short, anonymous questionnaires on their reactions to the scripts. Whatever responses you get from an audience, keep in mind that another audience may react differently to the same script.

If publicized by a news release to the media and flyers posted around town, the reading will attract a large enough audience to make its reactions to the scripts representative and potentially satisfying.

After extensive writing and perhaps public readings, you may be ready to try to see one of your best short scripts through to a video or film production. I stress extensive practice in writing because beginning scriptwriters and filmmakers often rush into production without a well-thought-out script. (Often first films and videos also lack competent photography, editing, sound, and appropriate and skilled performers; therefore, some are about as much fun to watch as listening to someone run a fingernail over a chalkboard.)

Turning your script over to others has advantages and disadvantages, but unless you are already experienced in directing, videotaping or filming, and editing, you will probably want experienced videomakers or filmmakers to take on the project. (It's wise to ask to look at samples of the director's or producer's previous work before turning over your script.) By letting others take over, you can continue to work on your writing and rewriting and not get caught up in and worn down by the technicalities of production.

The biggest disadvantage in handing your script to others, however, is that they may redo much of your work. Experienced scriptwriters will tell you that nearly everyone believes they can write scripts or at least rewrite them. So, if you do not produce or direct your script you will be wise to reach an agreement beforehand on how much control you'll keep over the story and how much the videomakers or filmmakers will have. (To better assure that their vision is brought to the screen, most experienced writers of short scripts insist that they direct the film and be involved in all aspects of the production.)

You may be fortunate: the collaboration may improve the story of your script. It will certainly change it. You should expect that and not get upset when the final product is not entirely what you visualized. If money is involved, you should also decide who spends what and who gets what income. For that, you may need an attorney to draw up a contract.

Once your script is produced, you will probably want to have your first showing for family and friends. After that, if you are happy with the production, you should help promote the finished film or video. Set up public showings and send a news release to the media, post flyers around town, and contact film and video teachers, film or video societies, and area clubs or groups that might be interested.

If galleries or museums offer video screenings, contact them and ask if they include original short narrative videos in their programs. Many do. Normally, you would submit a copy of your videotape and ask if it could be included in an upcoming program.

Whenever your film or video is shown publicly, try to see your work with audiences and observe their reactions. You may want to take notes on audience responses as they watch. If possible, you may invite the audience to stay after the showing and ask questions and make observations. Through such publicity and showings you gain recognition; you may also learn how your work affects viewers.

If you live in or near a city, you may want to see if it houses associations of independent filmmakers or videomakers. They can be an excellent source for information on workshops, contests, festivals, and (occasionally) money for productions. They may have a library, a members' newsletter, and limited production facilities. They can also be a source for meeting other filmmakers and videomakers.

In planning, writing, and rewriting short scripts and seeing them through to public readings and production and showings, you will develop your skills in writing scripts, gain the satisfaction of sharing your visions of life, and achieve the rewards of reaching others with perhaps the most powerful communications tool so far devised—the moving sights and living sounds of film and video. And, if you like, you'll be in stronger condition to write feature-length scripts. After you have learned to run miles, you may be ready for a marathon.

Glossary
Bibliography
Films and Videos
Distributors of Short Films
  and Videotapes
Index

Glossary

BEGINNING SCRIPTWRITERS SHOULD write—not try to direct as they write—and they need not learn technical terms to write effective scripts. In fact, such terms can get in the way of good writing and easy reading. In this glossary, therefore, I have defined only terms used in this book.

For additional terms explained in depth, see Ira Konigsberg's *The Complete Film Dictionary,* 2nd ed., and the revised edition of Frank Beaver's *Dictionary of Film Terms: The Aesthetic Companion to Film Analysis.*

Character. An imaginary person found in novels, short stories, plays, and fictional films. *Character* should be distinguished from *performer,* the person who re-creates or enacts a character.

Character biography. A description of a character's imaginary life before the story begins, during the story, and sometimes after the story. Created by some writers to help them understand their characters more completely.

Cut. The most common transition between shots, made by joining the end of one shot to the beginning of the following shot. When projected, the transition from one shot to the next appears instantaneous.

Cutting Continuity (Script). A written description of a finished film. May contain shot and scene divisions, descriptions of settings and actions, dialogue, camera angles and distances, occasionally even the duration of shots or scenes and the types of transitions between them.

Dialogue. Conversation between two or more characters.

Dissolve. A frequently used transition between shots in which the first shot begins to fade out as the next shot fades in, overlapping the first shot before replacing it. Often used between scenes or sequences to imply a change of location or a later time, or both.

Dolly. 1. A wheeled platform used to move a motion picture camera around while filming. 2. To film while the camera is mounted on a moving dolly or wheeled platform.

Editing. The selecting and arranging of the processed segments of photographed motion picture film or videotape. Editors, sometimes in consultation with the director, determine which shots to include, what is the most effective version of each shot, the arrangement and duration of shots, and transitions between them.

Establishing shot. A shot in which the camera seems to be a long distance from the subject, used at the beginning of a scene to "establish" or show where the action that is to follow takes place.

Exterior. A scene to be filmed outdoors.

Extreme long shot. Image in which the subject appears to be far from the camera.

Fade-in. Optical effect in which the image changes by degrees from darkness to illumination. Often used at the beginning of a scene or sequence.

Fade-out. Optical effect in which the image changes by degrees from illumination to darkness. Often used at the end of a shot. Often used at the conclusion of a sequence. Sometimes employed at the end of a film as a gradual exit from the world of the film.

Feature. A film, variously defined in length, but usually regarded as being at least sixty minutes long.

Flashback. A shot or few shots, brief scene, or (rarely) sequence that interrupts a story to show earlier events.

Freewriting. Spontaneous writing with minimal concern for grammar and spelling, used by writers to generate material that may be rewritten for later use.

Intercut. To alternate between two or more scenes in editing, often to make them appear to take place at the same time.

Interior. A scene to be filmed inside a building.

Master-scene format. Screenplay format that presents the script in scenes but not shots. A film script in the master-scene format includes any dialogue but usually excludes most directions about cinematography, mise en scène, editing, and sound.

Meaning. What a story shows in general about human behavior or—occasionally—about other living creatures or nature. Sometimes called "theme."

Mise en scène ("meez ahn sen," with a nasalized second syllable). A film's use of setting, subject (usually characters), lighting, and composition (the arrangement of setting and subjects within the frame).

Montage. A series of shots, usually combined by dissolves, used to present a condensation of events. In *The Resurrection of Broncho Billy* (chapter 6), a montage shows images of the old West as the old man tells Billy about past cowboy life.

Narration. The comments of an unseen person in a film.

O.S. The off-screen voice of a character.

Plot. See Structure.

Producer. The person in charge of the business and administrative aspects of making a film, typically including acquiring rights to the script and securing the personnel to make the film.

Production. The making of a film or video, the transformation of a film script into a film or video.

Rough cut. An early version of an edited film or videotape. Usually it is longer, less coherent, and less effective than the finished film.

Running time. The time that elapses when the complete film or video is shown at its intended speed. Nearly always the running time is much shorter than the story time.

Scene. A section of a narrative film that gives the impression of action taking place during one uninterrupted time and in one location. (If the action is uninterrupted but shifts to a new location, even if it is only beyond a door, a new scene begins.) See also Shot and Sequence.

Scene card. Note card, such as a three by five, used to briefly describe the setting, characters, and action of a scene. Often used in planning a screenplay.

Screenplay. In this book, an early version of a film or video script, a script written before filming begins.

Script. The general term for all written descriptions of a film: planned (screenplay), in production (shooting script or continuity), or finished (cutting continuity [script]).

Sequence. Often, and in this book, the word means a series of related consecutive scenes, perceived as a major unit of a film story.

Setting. The place where filmed action occurs. Often used to reveal character, mood, and meanings.

Shot. (1) A strip of processed motion picture film or videotape that when projected usually shows an uninterrupted action or an immobile subject during an uninterrupted passage of time. (2) As a verb it means filmed; for example, "they shot the scene at the train station."

Storyboard. A series of drawings accompanied by brief descriptions of each shot of a planned film or video story.

Story time. The time covered by the story of a film. Nearly always the story time of a film is much longer than its running time.

Structure. In a fictional film, "structure" can be thought of as the selection and arrangement of scenes or sequences. The actions are not necessarily chronological, though they usually are in a short film, and usually insignificant actions are omitted.

Symbol. Anything perceptible that has significance or meaning beyond its usual meaning or function, as in the first and last scenes of *Avenue X* (chapter 5).

Theme. See Meaning.

Treatment. A summary of a planned film story, usually written in paragraphs, occasionally with some dialogue.

Bibliography

BELOW ARE INCLUDED three types of sources: entries for works cited within this book, other useful printed sources for aspiring scriptwriters, and some Internet addresses for sources on short films or scriptwriting. For entries that are not self-explanatory I have included a brief annotation.

Bertagnolli, Olivia, and Jeff Rackham, eds. *Creativity and the Writing Process.* New York: John Wiley & Sons, 1982.
  A collection of essays grouped under seven headings: the creative process, concentration, inspiration, memory, faith, song, and technique.

Brady, John. *The Craft of the Screenwriter: Interviews with Six Celebrated Screenwriters.* New York: Simon and Schuster, 1982.
  An introductory essay and in-depth interviews with six successful writers of U.S. features. Of interest to beginning scriptwriters is the information on work habits and writing/revising techniques.

Brande, Dorothea. *Becoming a Writer.* Los Angeles: J. P. Tarcher, 1981.
  Includes chapters on the unconscious and conscious, harnessing the unconscious, writing on schedule, criticizing your own writing, and learning to see again.

Butler, Samuel. "On the Making of Music, Pictures, and Books." In *The Note-Books of Samuel Butler.* London: A.C. Fifield, 1918.

Cooper, Pat, and Ken Dancyger. *Writing the Short Film.* Newton, Mass.: Butterworth-Heinemann, 1994.
  Includes five short screenplays.

Dardon, Robert. "Cheap Tricks: How to Write a No-Budget Film." *The Independent Film and Video Monthly* 19, No. 4 (May 1996): 30–33.

Egri, Lajos. *The Art of Dramatic Writing: Its Basis in the Creative Interpretation of Human Motives.* New York: Simon and Schuster, 1960.
  Emphasizes writing plays with a central idea or premise, three-

dimensional characters in believable settings, and conflict to develop the characters and to advance plot. Although the book is not specifically about screenwriting and parts of it are dated, screenwriters can benefit from reading sections of it closely. This book is sometimes required reading in screenwriting courses.

Elbow, Peter. *Writing with Power: Techniques for Mastering the Writing Process.* New York: Oxford Univ. Press, 1981.
Parts on freewriting and sharing, More Ways of Getting Words on Paper, More Ways to Revise, Audience, Feedback, and Power in Writing.

Farrington, Jan. "Words and Pictures by . . . Writing for the Movies." *Writing!* 6, No. 8 (Apr. 1984): 3–17.

Froug, William. *The Screenwriter Looks at the Screenwriter.* New York: Delta, 1972.
Interviews with twelve American screenwriters.

———. *The New Screenwriter Looks at the New Screenwriter.* Los Angeles: Lone Eagle, 1991.
More interviews with screenwriters.

Goldman, William. *Adventures in the Screen Trade: A Personal View of Hollywood and Screenwriting.* Expanded ed. New York: Warner Books, 1983.
Mostly about writing feature films, yet parts of the book are useful to all beginning scriptwriters, especially six sections of part 1— Auteurs, Beginnings, Endings, Speed, Subtext, and Believing Reality—and the fourth and last part of the book, "Da Vinci," which includes Goldman's short story of that title, a description of his considerations before adapting it, the short screenplay adaptation, and responses to the screenplay by five professional filmmakers: a production designer, a cinematographer, an editor, a composer, and a director.

Hill, John. "Subject: Dialogue—Emotional vs. Corny." *The Journal* [of the Writers Guild of America, West] 6, No. 2 (Feb. 1993): 11.

Hull, Raymond. *How to Write a Play.* Cincinnati: Writer's Digest Books, 1983.
On how to write plays for local production and how to find producers and publishers; includes chapters on conflict, action, complications, and crises.

Johnson, Dirk. "A Storytelling Renaissance." *New York Times* (natl. ed.), 19 May 1986.

Knight, Damon. *Creating Short Fiction*. Cincinnati: Writer's Digest Books, 1981.
>Six parts: Developing Your Talent as a Writer, Idea into Story, Beginning a Story, Controlling a Story, Finishing a Story, and Being a Writer.

Levy, Edmond. *Making a Winning Short: How to Write, Direct, Edit, and Produce a Short Film*. New York: Henry Holt, 1994.
>Includes an original short script and information on how it was written then made into a short film.

Loch, Chuck. "How to Feed Your Brain and Develop Your Creativity." *Writer's Digest,* Feb. 1981, 20–22, 24–25.

Miller, William. "An Interview with Terrence McDonnell." *Journal of Film and Video* 36, No. 3 (Summer 1984): 51–57.
>McDonnell is an independent television screenwriter.

Minot, Stephen. *Three Genres: The Writing of Poetry, Fiction, and Drama,* 4th ed. Englewood Cliffs, N.J.: Prentice Hall, 1988.

Neeld, Elizabeth. *Yes! You Can Write*. Chicago: Nightingale-Conant Corporation, 1986.
>An audio cassette program, mainly focused on writing in business.

Norman, Marsha. "Ten Golden Rules for Playwrights." In Sylvia K. Burack, ed., *The Writer's Handbook*. Boston: The Writer, Inc., 1988.

O'Connor, Flannery. "Writing Short Stories." *Mystery and Manners*. New York: Farrar, Straus & Giroux, 1969.

Schemo, Diana Jean. "Where Screenwriters Can Get a Hearing." *New York Times* (natl. ed.), 13 Dec. 1994: B3.
>On public readings of film scripts.

Scheuer, Dorothy. "David Seltzer, Filmmaker." *Scholastic Update* 118 (16 May 1986): 27.

Stevens, William K. "For Those Who Have Lost Sleep, the First Casualty Is Creativity." *New York Times* (natl. ed.), 5 Jan. 1989.

Straczynski, J. Michael. "The Great Pretenders." *Writer's Digest* 64 (Feb. 1984): 64–66.

"Talk on Train Traps Suspect in a Shooting." *New York Times* (natl. ed.), 6 Feb. 1985.

Thoreau, Henry David. *The Writings of Henry David Thoreau,* 20 vols. Boston: Houghton Mifflin, 1906.

Ueland, Brenda. *If You Want to Write,* 2d ed. St. Paul, Minn.: Graywolf Press, 1987.
In part, the book argues that if you write honestly about something important to you and write at first without editing, then rewrite, you can write effectively, at least sometimes.

Van Dormael, Jaco [film director]. Interview. *Morning Edition,* National Public Radio. 19 Mar. 1992.

Walter, Richard. *Screenwriting: The Art, Craft and Business of Film and Television Writing.* New York: New American Library, 1988.

——. *The Whole Picture: Strategies for Screenwriting Success in the New Hollywood.* New York: Plume, 1997.

Internet Sources

The Independent Film Channel, which shows some short films:
http://www.ifctv.com

The Sundance Channel, which shows short films:
http://www.sundancechannel.com/channel

The Internet Film Network shows films that run as long as fifteen minutes:
http://www.ifilm.net

The Internet Movie Database includes reviews of some short films:
http://us.imdb.com

Links to many Web screenwriting sources, feature and short:
http://www-unix.oit.umass.edu/~norden/scm.html

Screenwriters and Playwrights Homepage:
http://www.teleport.com/~cdeemer/scrwriter.html

Films and Videos

WHAT FOLLOWS ARE brief descriptions of films I believe would be useful for aspiring writers of short scripts to view and study. The listing is far from complete. Films excluded from it are not necessarily unworthy: I have heard or read about many short films that seem to be well done but never had the opportunity to see them.

The films listed below were probably not unusually difficult to make: they have small casts, few or no special effects, and (mostly) ordinary locations. Included are films as long as thirty-four minutes.

It's a good idea to study some of these films, but if you lack access to these or other short films, studying the following brief descriptions will help you develop a sense of how much can be shown in a short film. The descriptions may also make you aware of the variety of subjects possible in the short film.

The following stories may be available in 16 mm film or videocassette from one or more of the following sources: public library film or video collections (free), or university audiovisual services (rental to public), or commercial film or video distributors (rental or sales). Unfortunately, your neighborhood video store probably has none of these titles.

For each film I have given the title and where appropriate any alternative titles, country, year of first release, running time, an indication whether the film is in color or black and white, producer or director or both, and writer(s). For films with untraditional sound tracks, I have indicated which components (narration, dialogue, sound effects, music) are included. For each film I have also given a brief, partial description of the story, though not, generally, the films' endings or my interpretation.

In each instance, I have studied the film described and not taken the word of catalogs and reference books. For information on film and video distributors, see "Distributors of Short Films and Videotapes" in the following section.

And You Act Like One, Too. U.S.A. 1976. 24 minutes. Black and white.
Directed and written by Susan Seidelman while she was a student at New York University.

223

On her thirtieth birthday, a young married woman wants to feel attractive, but the day's events frustrate her wish.

The screenplay for this film and an analysis of it were printed in the first edition of this book, pp. 64–88.

Avenue X. U.S.A. 1993. 15 ½ minutes. Shot in black and white and tinted amber. Written, produced, and directed by Leslie McCleave while at New York University, Graduate School of Film and Television.

Near Coney Island a young man is too worn out by his work to pay much attention to a boy who wants to show him something he had found at the beach.

The film is described by McCleave in chapter 5.

Board and Care. U.S.A. 1980. 27 minutes. Color. Directed, edited, and written by Ron Ellis.

A young man and woman who have Down's syndrome seek and briefly find friendship and love together, then are separated by their guardians.

The Children. See *Tamaita, O.*

Cigarettes & Coffee. U.S.A. 1992. 24 minutes. Color. Written and directed by Paul Anderson.

Most of the action occurs in a roadside restaurant. The film cuts back and forth between three story lines: a married couple on their honeymoon, a hired killer whose target we learn late in the film, and two men in a nearby booth: one believes his wife has been unfaithful and seeks advice from his friend about what he should do.

Cowgirl. U.S.A. 1996. 17 minutes. Color. Written and directed by Sunny Lee.

A young Asian-American woman is caught between cultures. She is infatuated with cowboy movies and with a particular cowboy, not with her devoted Asian-American friend, who the older generation of Asian-American women urge to marry the young woman.

The Dog Ate It. U.S.A. 1991. 27 minutes. Color. Written and directed by Steve Pearl while he was a student at Loyola Marymount University.

A satirical fantasy about a marginal student who despite major obstacles writes an inspiring term paper the night before it is due.

For Gentlemen Only. Canada 1976. 28 minutes. Color. Produced by the National Film Board of Canada. Directed by Michael Scott. Written by David King.

An aging man living in a run-down city hotel "for gentlemen only" becomes depressed that his well-ordered life will be changed by the hotel's renovation and admittance of women. His best friend finally does a rebellious act that helps draw him out of his depression.

Games. U.S.A. 1996. 14 minutes. Color. Written and directed by Stephanie Ripps while at New York University.

Filmed mostly in the Red Hook section of Brooklyn, *Games* depicts an hour in the life of a young Latino who comes to reject his older brother's macho ideas.

Homesick. U.S.A. 1989. 28 minutes. Color. Directed by Johanna Demetrakas. Written by Robert Gordon.

A man visits his grown son, daughter-in-law, and teenage grandson. To the teenager, Grandpa reveals that he is healthy and later plays cupid. But with the boy's parents Grandpa acts as if he were still incapacitated by a stroke because he prefers living in a nursing home to living with them.

Judgement. U.S.A. 1995. 30 $^1/_2$ minutes. Color. Written by Nelson McCormick and David Winkler. Directed by David Winkler.

The Judgement County (Texas) deputy sheriff only three months into the job faces an ambiguous but dangerous situation without the benefit of his more experienced boss. The suspect, who might be guilty and dangerous, comes under extreme danger himself.

Leon's Case. U.S.A. 1982. 25 minutes. Color. Directed by Daniel Attias. Written by Raymond Hartung while he was a student at the American Film Institute.

The often amusing story of the idealistic and sincere Leon Bernstein, who is "the last fugitive member of the Village 8" still thinking and acting as he did in the 1960s. He attempts to rally both the masses and his friends to protest the social injustices and militarism of the 1980s.

The screenplay for this film and an analysis of it were printed in the first edition of this book, pp. 19–63.

Les Mistons (*The Brats* or *The Mischief Makers*). France 1957. 18 minutes. Black and white. Director: François Truffaut. Adapted by Truffaut from "Virginales" by Maurice Pons. Narration and music but no dialogue.

An adult narrator tells of the times when he and four other adolescent boys admired and teased an attractive young woman.

Neighbors (French title: *Les Voisins*). Canada 1952. 8 minutes. Color and black-and-white prints available. The National Film Board of Canada. Director and writer: Norman McLaren. No dialogue and no narration but music and sound effects. Uses live action, animation, and pixillation (the actors are sometimes filmed in stop-motion photography).

Symbolic story of two men fighting over possession of a flower that has grown along the property line between them.

Night Ride. U.S.A. 1994. 29½ minutes. Color. Written and directed by Andrew Garrison. The script is based on a short story from *Kinfolks* by Gurney Norman.

In early 1960s eastern Kentucky, a man takes his fourteen-year-old nephew, who now lives with his deceased father's parents, "for a little ride on a spring evening," a time for companionship, the passing on of male traditions, and loving memories of the man's brother, the boy's miner father.

An Occurrence at Owl Creek Bridge. France 1962. 27 minutes. Black and white. Director: Robert Enrico. Adapted by Robert Enrico from the short story by Ambrose Bierce. No audible dialogue. No narration.

During the American Civil War, on a railroad bridge a civilian is hanged then seems to escape. A study of psychology and time using many filmmaking techniques.

The Other Side. Original title: *De Overkant,* Dutch for "the opposite side." Belgium 1966. 10 minutes. Black and white. Direction and script by Herman Wuyts. No dialogue. No narration. No music except during the opening credits and the final moments of the film. Only sound effect: occasional machine gun fire.

A symbolic story about masses of people in an unidentified town who are forced to keep their hands against the walls of buildings as they move slowly sideways. Eventually, some try to rebel.

This film was described and analyzed in the first edition of this book, pp. 102–7.

The Red Balloon (Le Ballon Rouge). France 1956. 34 minutes. Color. Directed and written by Albert Lamorisse. Music, random voices, street noises, but no dialogue.

In a section of Paris a boy finds a large red balloon, which magically takes on a life of its own and follows him. Later a gang of children tries to capture the balloon and finally does so. An ambiguous, symbolic child's fantasy that appeals to many people of all ages.

The Resurrection of Broncho Billy. U.S.A. 1970. 21 minutes. Sepia tint except for the last scene, which is in color. Produced by John Longenecker. Directed by James Rokos. Original screenplay by John Carpenter, Nick Castle, Trace Johnston, John Longenecker, and James Rokos. Made at the University of Southern California.

A young man lives in a city yet dresses and acts as if he were a movie cowboy.

The film is described in detail in chapter 6.

Strange Fruit. U.S.A. 1978. 32 minutes. Color. Produced and directed by Seth Pinsker for the American Film Institute. Writer: Stephen Katz, based loosely on the novel *Strange Fruit* by Lillian Smith.

In a small town in 1948 Georgia, a young black man who tries just to do his job and be left alone decides to register to vote, although it is dangerous for him to do so.

The String Bean. Original title: *Le Haricot*, which is French for a type of bean. France 1962. 17 minutes. Part black and white; part color. Director and writer: Edmond Séchan. Uninterrupted instrumental music and occasional sound effects, but no dialogue and no narration.

The story of an aged woman living in a section of Paris who tries to grow a plant from a bean.

This film was described and analyzed in the first edition of this book, pp. 89–101.

O Tamaita (*The Children*). New Zealand 1996. 14 minutes. Black and white. Written and directed by Sima Urale. Minimal dialogue.

The children of a large Samoan family are left largely to the supervision of the eldest child while both parents work. Told from the children's point of view; for example, no adult face is seen clearly or for long.

That Burning Question. U.S.A. 1990. 27 minutes. Black and white. Written and directed by Alan Taylor while at New York University.

A young man and his girlfriend and another young male friend search for a man who has threatened to immolate himself because the woman he loves has spurned him.

Trouble. U.S.A. 1995. 16 minutes. Black and white. Written and directed by Carrie Blank while at New York University.

A bright eleven-year-old living in Queens with her mother has her own fantasy worlds and a big secret while her mother has suffered many disappointments with her four daughters and is into denial.

Two Men and a Wardrobe (*Dwaj Ludzie z Szafa*). Poland 1957. 15 minutes. Black and white. Direction and script by Roman Polanski, who also makes a brief appearance in the film as the young man who beats up one of the men carrying the wardrobe. Instrumental music and occasional sound effects but no dialogue or narration.

A symbolic story of two men who emerge from the sea carrying a bulky wardrobe with a mirror. In a town, they and their wardrobe are repeatedly rejected; one of the men is beaten. They pass near but do not see theft, cruelty to animals, drunkenness, and murder. Still lugging the wardrobe, they return to the sea.

The Ways of Harmony. U.S.A. 1995. 17 minutes. Color. Written and directed by Christopher Grant while he was a student at New York University.

An interracial couple face an awkward moment in their marriage when they come to argue over a small piano delivered to the base of their Brooklyn stoop.

When the Bough Breaks. U.S.A. 1983. 30 minutes. Color. Producer: American Film Institute. Director: Ellen Sandler. Writers: Dennis Danziger and Ellen Sandler, based loosely on the short story "A Family Affair" by John L'Heureux.

A teenage girl growing up in a small town finds that her desire for independence and romance conflicts with her widowed father's desire to control her.

Distributors of Short Films
and Videotapes

ELOW IS A SELECTED list of organizations that produce, rent, or sell
16 mm prints or VHS tapes of short fictional films. (If you are seeking
a distributor for a short fictional film you have made, some of the organizations listed below would welcome your enquiry.) Many film and
video distributors change addresses or phone numbers often or go out
of business or merge, so for their current addresses and phone numbers
consult the most recent edition of *Index to 16 mm Educational Films,*
Educational Film/Video Locator, The Video Source Book, or *Variety's*
Complete Home Video Directory. Those sources also tell which distributors rent a particular film or videotape.

Aims Multimedia Inc.
9710 DeSoto Ave.
Chatsworth, CA 91311
E-mail: dss@aims-multimedia.com
tel.: 800-367-2467; in California: 818-773-4300
fax: 818-341-6700
Web site: http://www.aims-multimedia.com

Apollo Cinema Corporation
1160 Alvira Street
Los Angeles, CA 90035
E-mail: apollocinema@earthlink.net
tel.: 323-939-1122
fax: 323-939-1133

Carousel Film and Video
260 Fifth Ave., Suite 905
New York, NY 10001
E-mail: carousel@pipeline.com

tel.: 800-683-1660; in New York: 212-683-1660
fax: 212-683-1662
(video sales and some rental)

cinéBLAST!/Cinema Parallel
601 River Road
Sykesville, MD 21784
E-mail: cineblast@cinemaparallel.com
tel.: 800-860-8896; in New York: 212-533-0868
web site: http://www.cinemaparallel.com
(cinéBLAST! is a series of video collections of short films, including fictional films.)

Coe Film Associates, Inc.
65 E. 96th Street
New York, NY 10128
E-mail: cfainc1@juno.com
tel.: 212-831-5355
fax: 212-996-6728
(distributes short films to TV and other markets)

Indiana University
Instructional Support Services/Media Resources
Franklin Hall 0001
601 East Kirkwood
Bloomington, IN 47405-1223
E-mail: issmedia@indiana.edu
tel.: 800-552-8620; in Indiana: 812-855-8765
fax: 812-855-8404
web site: http://www.indiana.edu/~mediares/catalog.htm

ITVS (Independent Television Service)
51 Federal Street, Suite 401
San Francisco, CA 94107
E-mail: itvs@itvs.org
tel.: 415-356-8383
fax: 415-356-8391
web site: http://www.itvs.org

Paulist Productions
P.O. Box 1057
17575 Pacific Coast Highway
Pacific Palisades, CA 90272-1057
tel.: 800-624-8613; in California: 310-454-0688
fax: 310-459-6549
(sales of videos and 16 mm films)

Phoenix Learning Group
2349 Chaffee Drive
St. Louis, MO 63146
tel.: 800-221-1274; in St. Louis: 314-569-0211
fax: 314-569-2834

Pyramid Media
Box 1048
Santa Monica, CA 90406-1048
E-mail: www.pyramidmedia.com
tel.: 800-421-2304; in California: 310-828-7577
fax: 310-453-9083
(sales and rental of video and 16mm film)

Short Cinema Journal (DVDs that include short fictional films)
1041 N. Mansfield Ave., 2nd Floor
Los Angeles, CA 90038
E-mail: my2cents@dvdmags.com
tel.: 323-993-1919
fax: 323-993-9689
web site: http://www.dvdmags.com

Such Media
Post Office Box 1234
Okemos, MI 48805-1234
E-mail: nextgenvideo@yahoo.com
tel.: 800-670-9282; in Michigan: 517-349-5554
fax: 517-349-0602
web site: http://www.suchmedia.com
(video sales only)

Tapestry International
920 Broadway, Suite 1501
New York, NY 10010
E-mail: tapintl@aol.com
tel.: 212-505-2288
(distributes short films and videos to TV and home video companies)

University of California
Center for Media and Independent Learning
2000 Center Street, Suite 400
Berkeley, CA 94704
E-mail: cmil@uclink.berkeley.edu
tel.: 510-642-0460
fax: 510-643-9271
web site: http://www-cmil.unex.berkeley.edu/media

Women Make Movies, Inc.
462 Broadway, Suite 500 K
New York, NY 10013-2618
E-mail: info@wmm.com
tel.: 212-925-0606
fax: 212-925-2052

Index